THE SECRET
OF THE
STRATEMEYER SYNDICATE

RECOGNITIONS

Mystery Writers

Bruce Cassiday, General Editor

Raymond Chandler by Jerry Speir
P. D. James by Norma Siebenheller
John D. MacDonald by David Geherin
*Victorian Masters of Mystery: From Wilkie Collins
to Conan Doyle*
by Audrey Peterson
Ross Macdonald by Jerry Speir
The Murder Mystique: Crime Writers on Their Art
edited by Lucy Freeman
*Roots of Detection: The Art of Deduction
before Sherlock Holmes*
edited by Bruce Cassiday
Dorothy L. Sayers by Dawson Gaillard
Sons of Sam Spade: The Private Eye Novel in the 70s
by David Geherin
*Murder in the Millions: Erle Stanley Gardner—
Mickey Spillane—Ian Fleming*
by J. Kenneth Van Dover
Rex Stout by David R. Anderson
Dashiell Hammett by Dennis Dooley
The American Private Eye: The Image in Fiction
by David Geherin
John le Carré by Peter Lewis
13 Mistresses of Murder by Elaine Budd

THE SECRET
OF THE
STRATEMEYER SYNDICATE

Nancy Drew, The Hardy Boys,
and the
Million Dollar Fiction Factory

Carol Billman

THE UNGAR PUBLISHING COMPANY
New York

Library of Congress Cataloging-in-Publication Data

Billman, Carol.
  The secret of the Stratemeyer Syndicate.

  Bibliography: p.
  Includes index.
  1. Stratemeyer, Edward, 1862–1930 — Criticism and
interpretation. 2. Stratemeyer Syndicate. 3. Children's
literature in series. 4. Children's stories, American —
History and criticism. 5. Drew, Nancy (Fictitious
character) 6. Hardy Boys (Fictitious characters)
I. Title.
PS3537.T817Z56   1986   813'.52   86-5546
ISBN 0-8044-2055-6

For my chums,
Will and Lorna

CONTENTS

LIST OF ILLUSTRATIONS

ACKNOWLEDGMENTS

To write a book about a literary canon as big as that of Edward Stratemeyer and his Syndicate requires some sleuthing in itself, especially when the books in question have often been deemed forgettable and best forgotten. Along the trail of the Stratemeyer Syndicate series mysteries I have been aided and guided by a number of able assistants, especially John M. Kelly, Curator of the deGrummond Collection at the University of Southern Mississippi, and the staffs of the Free Library of Philadelphia and the Library of Congress. Then there were all the public librarians from New Orleans to Newark, Delaware, who, while not always approving of my selections, cheerfully checked out and renewed for me scores of series books — and my mother, Mary Billman, who showed her skill in turning up early titles in the Hardy Boys and Nancy Drew series.

I also wish to thank Nancy Axelrad, a current partner at the Stratemeyer Syndicate, for taking time to answer my questions about the Syndicate's history and Bruce Cassiday at Frederick Ungar Publishing Co. for his good suggestions about how to manage the sprawling Stratemeyer output in one book. And finally I thank my husband, Will Norman, for his dogged efforts at photographing cheaply printed and sometimes crumbling books wherever we found them.

From the bushes along the road sprang several masked figures.

—*Tom Swift and His Electric Runabout*
Victor Appleton
Grosset and Dunlap, 1910

1

THE RISE OF SERIES FICTION

Dear Readers:

Some writers are remembered chiefly for one book that stormed the public's imagination — Harriet Beecher Stowe and Margaret Mitchell owe their places in the realm of common knowledge to *Uncle Tom's Cabin* and *Gone with the Wind*, respectively. Other best-selling authors, like television scriptwriters, are prolific but obscure, perhaps by choice when they adopt a pen name. How many remember who wrote the Little Colonel books or the Uncle Wiggily stories or the Raggedy Ann and Andy series? This book is about a writer and literary entrepreneur who falls within the latter group who have been eclipsed by their outpouring: Edward Stratemeyer.

No matter that Stratemeyer's beloved Rover Boys books for boys, begun in 1899, had sold an estimated five million copies by 1930, the year of the author's death. Nor that he created and then presided over a literary "syndicate," his own term, that can be compared with the Dumas fiction factory in nineteenth-century Paris. The fact remains that not many people, beyond book collectors and students of children's literature, connect Stratemeyer's name with the Bobbsey Twins, Bomba the Jungle Boy, the Boys of Columbia High, Christopher Cool/TEEN Agent, Dave Dashaway, Doris Force, the Happy Hollisters, the Hardy Boys, Honey Bunch, the Jerry Ford Wonder Stories, the Motion Picture Chums, Nancy Drew, the Outdoor Girls, the Rover

Boys, Ruth Fielding, Tom Swift, Kay Tracey, and the X Bar
X Boys. And these are but a small fraction of the greater and
lesser products—many actually written, or at least outlined and
edited, by Stratemeyer himself—of a writing mill that has turned
out over thirteen hundred books, with sales estimated at two hundred million copies.[1]

Despite his relative obscurity, Stratemeyer was not a secretive man. In fact, from the outset of his career he indulged himself
in correspondence to his readership, in the form of chatty introductory letters that began with "My Dear Lads," "Young
Friends," or some other affectionate salutation. The prefatory
epistles reveal (and it takes no supersleuth to puzzle out the
revelation, for he speaks without the veil of subtlety) the character
and values of the man. Stratemeyer admires boys who are "manly" and "wideawake"—the adjectives appear time and again—
and promotes such pastimes as motoring, baseball, and hunting.
Whether the letter was signed "Capt. Ralph Bonehill," "Arthur
M. Winfield," "Lester Chadwick," "Frank Webster," or Edward
Stratemeyer, the personality behind the print is the same.

These personalized but highly conventional introductions
also alert Stratemeyer's readers to what they might expect from
the book they have in hand. In his very first successful hardcover
novel, for example, Stratemeyer makes clear his twofold purpose
in writing a historical adventure about the Spanish-American
War:

> to present to young readers a simple and straightforward state-
> ment concerning the several causes leading up to the war with
> Spain and . . . to tell, in as interesting a fashion as the writer
> could command, the haps and mishaps of a sturdy, conscien-
> tious American lad, of good moral character and honest Chris-
> tian aim, who, compelled through the force of circumstances
> to make his own way in the world, becomes a sailor boy, a
> castaway, and then a gunner's assistant on the flagship *Olym-
> pia*.[2]

It seems in keeping with the subject, then, that this introductory
chapter map out precisely what awaits readers of *The Secret of the
Stratemeyer Syndicate*.

This study aims to describe and account for the staggering success of Stratemeyer's series, specifically his mystery series. And the success of the Syndicate is staggering, as the statistics already given suggest. Numerous Stratemeyer publications consistently sold like hotcakes, year in and year out. Some were so popular that children of the original protagonist(s) were created to carry on the tradition for new generations of readers—namely, the sons of the Rover Boys and Tom Swift, Jr. To cite figures for the champion series, Nancy Drew, it is remarkable that in six weeks during the Depression Christmas season of 1933, Macy's sold six thousand titles. (Incidentally, the runner-up in the figures that year was another Stratemeyer series, Bomba, with 3750 sales.) Fifty years later, nearly eighty million copies of Nancy Drew have been sold, several million more than her closest competitor, the Hardy Boys. Along the way she has generated such spin-offs as four feature-length films in the 1930s; a Parker Brothers board game in the late 1950s; a television series in the 1970s; and, within the last five years, two coloring books, a cookbook, a "private eye diary," and a date book. Nancy Drew, moreover, has gone international, having been translated into more than a dozen languages.[3]

When Edward Stratemeyer wrote the first title of the Drew series in 1929 shortly before his death, he had no clue as to the magnitude of the superstar he was introducing. Indeed, the success of his earlier suspense series seemed to surprise even him, an unshakable optimist. In the letter preceding the fifteenth story in his Rover Boys series, Stratemeyer confesses:

> Twelve years ago the line was started with the publication of the first three stories. . . . I earnestly hoped that the young people would like the tales, but never did I anticipate the tremendously enthusiastic welcome which was given to the volumes from the start, nor the steady sales, ever increasing, which has accompanied the series up to the present time.[4]

Later he would proclaim "astonishing" the fact that publishers had sold three and a half million copies of the books.[5]

The Stratemeyer corpus is not a freakish outcrop of cheap reading thrills for the young, a lonely counterpart to all the popular pulp magazines for adults like *Spicy Detective*, *Detective Story*, and *Ranch Romances*. Stratemeyer and the Syndicate's amazing output of some 125 series was exemplary, but it was also representative of the workings of the juvenile publishing world after the turn of the century. Stratemeyer's major publishers — Cupples and Leon, for one, and Grosset and Dunlap — issued a bevy of other series for young readers that held their own in the sales department. In the period from 1915 to 1930, for example, Grosset and Dunlap put out Percy Keese Fitzhugh's Tom Slade Scout Series, a deliberate competitor to Stratemeyer. Other houses — Lee and Shepard, Reilly and Britton, Henry Altemus, Whitman, Donohue, Appleton, and especially A. L. Burt — also capitalized on the series book phenomenon that crescendoed in the first decade of this century, remained immensely vital up to World War II, and lives on quite successfully today. Like the flops on the Stratemeyer record, some of the series produced by these and other houses never attained the popularity of the Stratemeyer stars or Street and Smith's Frank Merriwell books; and those that were once popular have for the most part faded in the public memory. Not many today can recall the Grammar School Boys, the Submarine Chums, the Khaki Girls, or Aunt Jane's Nieces, notwithstanding the fact that the last named came from the pen of L. Frank Baum, who earned his literary reputation by creating another series, the Oz fantasy books.[6] Still, the twentieth-century adventure series for young readers comprise a bona fide tradition — a craze, one could go so far as to say — that deserves resurrection and consideration. And Stratemeyer was the king of the emerging suspense series genre.

This "craze" led by Stratemeyer and the writers who worked for him, it must be pointed out, did not constitute radical reform in the field of children's book publication. The Syndicate's offerings follow in many ways the patterns of publication and fictional preferences that developed in the 1800s, the embryonic period of children's literature in America. Stratemeyer actually completed, after the death of their originators, the novels of two nineteenth-century giants in children's fiction: William T. Adams (Oliver Optic, pseud.) and Horatio Alger, Jr. And his later series fiction shows the influence of both Alger's heavy-handed style and his "gospel of virtue" value system. As for the elements of mystery and suspense in Stratemeyer's post-1900 work, they harken back to another immensely popular literary series, the Nick Carter tales of the 1880s and 1890s, penned by a variety of writers for Street and Smith's dime weekly publications . . . among whom was the omnipresent Stratemeyer.[7]

Likewise, the Stratemeyer series for girls and those for younger readers of both sexes, especially ones started in the first decade of this century like the Bobbsey Twins and Dorothy Dale, look back to the juvenile domestic series that flourished after the Civil War — e.g., Rebecca Clarke's (Sophie May, pseud.) Dotty Dimple and Little Prudy books begun in 1863; Martha Finley's (Martha Farquaharson, pseud.) twenty-eight-title Elsie Dinsmore series begun in 1867; Louisa May Alcott's books about the March girls, the first appearing in serial form in 1867; and Harriet M. Lothrop's (Margaret Sidney, pseud.) twelve Five Little Peppers books begun in 1880.[8] Even a Syndicate series begun in the 1920s, the Barton Books for Girls, was described by Cupples and Leon publicists as having a "style . . . somewhat of a reminder of that of Louisa M. Alcott, but thoroughly up-to-date in plot and action."

Stratemeyer, then, played on the success of the already popular idea of multiple-book fiction for boys and girls. What is more, his contemporaries' contributions to the series format helped to imprint the pattern indelibly in children's book writing and publishing. Today one finds, in addition to the ongoing Stratemeyer titles, such carry-over concepts as biographical and historical adventure series being initiated anew; first-rate fantastic fiction being published in series (for example, the work of Susan Cooper, Eleanor Cameron, and Madeleine L'Engle); and a host of mystery, adventure, and romance series that are the direct descendants of Stratemeyer and others.

The Stratemeyer suspense books are more than timely follow-ups to adventure series of the preceding century. His success can be attributed to two major departures from the old tradition. First, Stratemeyer's series depicted, as the publicists' blurb above puts it, "up-to-date" action and characters who enjoyed the freedoms and privileges of a new era. Most notably, the protagonists acted, like all those figures who leave home at the beginning of fairy tales, without any real adult supervision, while so many of the nineteenth-century heroes and heroines were ever so firmly guarded. Jacob Abbott, for example, in the 1830s created a series for boys that featured a young traveling protagonist named Rollo; but Rollo traveled in the company of his uncle, Mr. George, whose history and geography lessons could dampen trips to the most exciting places. Even those characters out on their own, like Alger's Dick Hunter and Tom Thatcher, lived under the aegis of a stern and pious master, the author, who duly commented on and drew moral conclusions about his boys' conduct at every narrative turn.

Flesh-and-blood boys, prototypes for the adventurous figures in Stratemeyer's boys' series, can be found in the popular children's fiction of the later 1800s. There was, in fact, a strain of "bad boy books," which began with Thomas Bailey Aldrich's *The Story of a Bad Boy* in 1870 and continued in such novels as George Wilbur Peck's *Peck's Bad Boy and His Pa* in 1883. But these characters were not really bad; they were merely cantankerous. Nor were they particularly bold, and certainly they were not liberated from adult supervision.[9] Stratemeyer's fiction depicted freewheeling youth who lived in the present and sported such contemporary luxury items as motor boats, automobiles, motorcycles, or . . . airplanes. There is no mistaking the old-fashioned, Algerian social and moral codes Stratemeyer maintained as underpinnings in his narratives; but, compared to preceding literature, these value systems did just that — underlay, or took a back seat to, the wonderful, superficial stories of adventure and suspense.

The Stratemeyer girls' series scream female high spirits brought on by a new era of women's rights, culminating, of course, in 1920 when women gained voting privileges. The mood as well as the action in Stratemeyer's books is unmistakably different from that in popular series for young female readers of the 1800s. Domestic hardship and suffering prevail in the excruciatingly sentimental Elsie Dinsmore books, which center on a beautiful, young (though she grows up to be a grandmother by the end of the series) heroine who endures and thereby triumphs over the machinations of her family. Chaucer's Griselda was no more patient or pious. Other best sellers, like the Five Little Peppers and Alcott's Little Women books, came close to

Farquaharson's Elsie novels in melodrama and sentiment. Even after 1900 the socially and morally conservative domestic tear-jerker sold well — for example, Eleanor Porter's *Pollyanna* of 1913 and *Rebecca of Sunnybrook Farm*, a much better novel written by Kate Douglas Wiggin in 1904. Occasionally there surfaced in these girls' books a tomboy who preferred adventure to handiwork and suffering: Alcott's Jo March or Sarah Chauncey Woolsey's Katy Carr in the contemporary *What Katy Did* and its sequels, written under the pen name Susan Coolidge. But it was not until the twentieth-century series (especially those appearing in the teens and thereafter) that girls were out on the roads and playing fields, up in the air, and at the war front — right there along with the boys involved in suspenseful adventures outside the home. It is no wonder that until these series by Stratemeyer and others took off girls' books consistently undersold counterparts for young males and girls themselves were driven to reading the more palatable fare published for boys.[10]

The second innovation in Stratemeyer's series concerns the extension and definition he (and his contemporary writers, it must always be added) supplied for the juvenile adventure story form. It is an interesting coincidence that he began his first blockbuster series, the Rover Boys, in 1899, just one year before the appearance of Baum's *The Wonderful Wizard of Oz*, a bellwether book in the previously motley field of American fantastic fiction for the young.[11]

Regarding girls' fiction, the achievement, as already discussed, was really a matter of extension. Heroines were lifted out of domestic dramas, out from under rigid familial supervision, first by being sent off to school and later through self-initiated undertakings. During the Stratemeyer Syndicate's golden years in the teens and twenties, girls' series fiction mirrored boys' books; both presented characters bound up in a sequence of adventures that, as the years passed, showed greater integration and direction and an escalation of Gothic suspense. And with the development of the Nancy Drew mysteries came, for the first time, a girls' series that outperformed contemporary boys' books in sales. Later, beginning with series that originated the 1930s, girls' books in an updated way came full circle; they reintroduced either a domestic or romantic plot into what could be called the "career mystery." The Stratemeyer Syndicate perhaps suggested this trend with its earlier Ruth Fielding line; the Syndicate's chief publisher, Grosset and Dunlap, led the way through the publication of such series as Judy Bolton, Cherry Ames, Connie Blair, and Vicki Barr.

What Stratemeyer, his subordinates, and his competitors did for the adventure story form in boys' literature requires special comment. Boys' fiction in the 1800s can be described, simply, as the adventure tale, which John Cawelti has called the oldest and most widely appealing of all popular story types. He elaborates:

> The central fantasy of the adventure story is that of the hero
> . . . overcoming obstacles and dangers and accomplishing some
> important and moral mission. Often, though not always, the
> hero's trials are the result of the machinations of a villain, and,
> in addition, the hero frequently receives, as a kind of side
> benefit, the favors of one or more attractive young ladies. . . .
> The true focus of interest in the adventure story is the character
> of the hero and the nature of the obstacles he has to over-
> come.[12]

This description fits what looks to be a varied assortment of books published for nineteenth-century boys. There was the moralistic adventure produced by Jacob Abbott and "Peter Parley" (Samuel Goodrich). After midcentury, such writers as "Oliver Optic," "Harry Castlemon" (Charles Fosdick), Charles C. Coffin, Edward S. Ellis, Kirk Munroe, Hezekiah Butterworth, and Noah Brooks served up travel adventures of a more swashbuckling and exciting nature set on the high seas, in the Wild West, in an earlier historical time, or a distant place. Stratemeyer himself began by writing these last two types of adventure. Then there were Alger's tales of "vertical" travel: his characters were "Bound to Rise," as one title put it, upward through the well-defined strata of American society, but only after surmounting a host of tangible and cultural obstacles.[13]

Stratemeyer and the other twentieth-century inheritors of this adventure story legacy popularized new subgenres of juvenile adventure fiction, in which emphasis shifted from the character of the hero and the obstacles besetting him to the story line itself:

school/sports novels (these two oftentimes went hand in hand); science adventure; war series; and, finally, the mystery, the ingredients of which eventually pervaded many of the other categories.[14] Furthermore, by virtue of the vast quantity of series books produced for young readers between 1900 and the end of World War II, the conventions of these subcategories of the basic adventure tale in time crystallized and were reduced to easily recognizable and repeatable formulas.

This summary reveals the sizeable proportions of Stratemeyer's bibliography. Selective treatment is demanded, for clarity's sake. Attention is focused in the chapters that follow on a handful of the Stratemeyer Syndicate's most representative and most popular series. Chapter 3 looks at Stratemeyer's personal favorite, the Rover Boys series, at the top of sales charts throughout the first quarter of this century. Both sets of Rover Boys books, *pères et fils*, demonstrate over the course of their development Stratemeyer's unique status as a transitional writer who, on the one hand, worked squarely within the kind of simple and moralistic adventure story he inherited from Alger and, on the other, experimented with new patterns of suspense. The fourth chapter considers my favorite Stratemeyer heroine, Ruth Fielding, whose series was the longest running and most prolific of the girls' fiction begun in the first two decades of the 1900s. At the outset, Ruth, an orphan in the grand tradition of so many of the sentimental heroines in nineteenth-century girls' books, labors through a set of domestic crises and adventures; but quickly and surely she moves on to the school scene, where she gradually blossoms as a noteworthy detective (and talented playwright!). Later, she takes her sleuthing and her career out into the wide world. The next two chapters are analyses of Stratemeyer's all-time best sellers, the Hardy Boys and Nancy Drew, initiated in 1927 and 1930, respectively. These two series exemplify the juvenile mystery genre in bold and formulaic relief: the fast action of chases on land and sea and sometimes underground, the code-breaking and intrepid detectives, the stereotypical villains, the inescapable clues—the footprints are always fresh—and a secure if crime-ridden setting where justice surely triumphs and the hero/heroine is resoundingly commended by one and all. Chapter 7 studies a popular Stratemeyer mystery series of the 1950s and 1960s, the Happy Hollisters written by "Jerry West" (not the basketball player). This series is the last successful addition to a long list of Stratemeyer offerings — most of which could be classified as family adventures in the old Five Little Peppers tradition — for young readers of both sexes. The admixture of mystery to the clearly established pattern of a domestic tale involving a host of siblings shows the extent to which the trappings and narrative formulas of detective fiction came to permeate other kinds of popular fiction for children.

These chapters that deal with the literary, sociocultural, and psychological attractions of five particularly popular and important Stratemeyer juvenile mystery series are surrounded by two others. In the second chapter, there is an overview of the Stratemeyer operation, including accounts of Edward Stratemeyer's life and literary dreams and of the efficient assembly-line production of the series, the steps of which were as formulaic as the products themselves. Chapter 8 likewise looks at the workings of the Syndicate, offering an explanation for the longevity of the Stratemeyer organization and its output in the versatility and flexibility evidenced throughout its history — in well-timed print and video follow-ups to successful series, in experimental or hybrid adventure formats, and in the Syndicate's willingness to revise its most popular mystery series. The concluding chapter also aims to explore further earlier explanations of the popularity of Stratemeyer's best-selling mystery and suspense series in terms of the fundamental readerly appeals of the mystery story — and especially of Stratemeyer's own packaging of the genre for the young.

Why focus on Stratemeyer's *mysteries*, instead of Baseball Joe, Bomba, and Tom Swift? There are two justifications. First, it is time that detective fiction be looked at with an eye to the personal reading history of the mystery buff as well as in light of the genre's more public literary historical development. The latter — that is, the literary history of popular mystery fiction as it originated in Poe's stories and Cooper's character Leatherstocking, on through Wilkie Collins' and Sir Arthur Conan Doyle's writing, and on to the great twentieth-century practitioners — has itself been a popular subject of investigation since midcentury. But the mysteries read early in their lives by four generations of Americans haven't been brought into the picture that emerges of a lively and fertile period for American literature of detection after the turn of the century. Since it is in childhood, starting with the highly patterned fairy tales, that readers acquire a taste for popular narrative formulas and begin to develop their literary habits and preferences, it seems important to consider juvenile fiction as part of readers' cultural heritage regarding the mystery genre.

Often, in fact, it is impossible to separate the strains of "adult" and "juvenile" mystery fiction. Students of detective fiction have traced connections between the pulp magazine mysteries so popular among adults in the 1920s and the dime novels and weekly magazines that appeared after 1860, first as western adventures but increasingly as detective stories by the 1880s and 1890s. Put simply, the first pulp was born in 1896 when Frank A. Munsey changed the paper his boys' magazine, *The Argosy*, was printed on. Now the dime novels, though not specifically written for boys, had been eagerly seized up by adolescents looking for relief from Alger or "Oliver Optic." The contribution made by Edward Stratemeyer to the Nick Carter weekly dime detective stories in the early 1890s has already been pointed out — in actuality he wrote twenty-two of the episodes — and with this experience he went on to create mystery series explicitly for boys. Thus the boys' series mysteries and the adult whodunits in *Black Mask* and other pulps have the same family tree.

Russel Nye has stated the relationship between the two kinds of mystery publication in another way:

> Stratemeyer shrewdly recognized that what interested the general reading public would also interest youngsters, and so constructed his books. . . . They were, in effect, watered down popular pulps, geared to the adolescent mind.[15]

It is, then, certainly no coincidence that the Hardy Boys and all their look-alike Stratemeyer contemporaries throughout the 1920s and 1930s (the X Bar X Boys, Perry Pierce, Roy Stover, the Nat Ridley Rapid Fire Detective Stories, among others) belong to a milestone epoch in American detective fiction for adults. The boys' detective books are the timely offspring of work by such writers as "S. S. Van Dine," the creators of "Ellery Queen," Dashiell Hammett, Erle Stanley Gardner, and then Raymond Chandler . . . soft-boiled though they may seem by comparison.

Similarly, the girls' series mysteries of the 1920s and 1930s and the popular mysteries for grown-ups by writers like Mrs. Charles Rohlfs (Anna Katherine Green, pseud.) and Mary Roberts Rinehart are both liberated descendants of the moralized domestic fiction read by girls and women in the 1800s. That is, Nancy Drew looks back to Elsie Dinsmore as Rinehart's heroines do to Jane Eyre: the difference is that the twentieth-century characters solve mysteries about haunted houses, rather than being confined to such settings and the worlds of domesticity they stand for.[16] The Stratemeyer girls' mysteries — from Ruth Fielding on to Nancy Drew, Doris Force, the Dana Girls, and Kay Tracey — also resemble their adult counterparts. Green's child-sized detective Violet Strange because of her influential father leads a double life as a socialite and working detective, a situation similar to that of Nancy Drew. And a recent reading of Rinehart's best-selling *The Circular Staircase* shows that it is not in title only that her fiction provided a model for Stratemeyer's Gothicized mystery series for girls. Finally, the career girl detectives that later dominated the girls' book scene have (with some major differences in their outlooks, to be sure) adult corollaries in currently popular detectives like Kate Fansler in the novels of Carolyn Heilbrun (Amanda Cross, pseud.) and Jemimah Shore in Lady Antonia Fraser's *Quiet as a Nun* and its sequels.

The second justification for concentrating on Stratemeyer's mystery series is their importance in Stratemeyer's own immense juvenile canon and within the larger context of children's literature. Stratemeyer's original contribution to children's series books was the further specification of the basic adventure story. Most significantly, Stratemeyer made the underlying premise of the mystery/suspense genre — the discovery of hidden and usually unlawful secrets — the motive for the protagonist's action throughout the narrative. It is true that Stratemeyer developed other kinds of popular adventure narratives, notably the sports adventure and the science adventure, and extended the earlier success, the travel tale, to new exotic dimensions in series like Don Sturdy,

Ted Scott the Flying Ace, and Bomba. But the series detective novel is his key success, and its story patterns have spilled over onto these other adventure genres from the days of Tom Swift on. The Syndicate even reintroduced the western within a mystery format in the 1960s.

If one takes as the sine qua non of the mystery what Jacques Barzun has described as the "ancient riddle of who is who [as it] unravels itself to an accompaniment of . . . wisdom"[17] — more broadly, the discovery of secrets — then it becomes apparent that the narrative of detection merely exemplifies with its dramatic formulas what happens any time a reader progresses through a story: the encountering of mysterious information within the book and the eventual discovery of what underlies these secrets. As Dennis Porter claims, the act of opening a book is akin to peeking into a treasure box full of the unknown.[18] The reader then moves through the book, constantly looking both backward and forward, taking knowledge he has gained and using it to make guesses about what is still a mystery, then revising his guesses as he reads further and comes upon more narrative evidence about the true direction and final outcome of the story.[19]

For young readers, it would seem, mystery fiction represents an especially clear case of what any reading of a story involves. The process of reading is still an uncertain enough proposition. Thus the series mystery — replete with characters who are unmistakably good or evil, easily recognized clues as to the crime's solution and to the way the story is told as well (for example, cliffhanging chapter endings), and a writing style that is both familiar and undemanding — offers extraordinary inducements for apprentice readers just coming to feel at home with the idea and act of reading a novel. There is even a seductive charm to the larger series framework in which these mysteries appear. Selma Lanes writes:

> Like the vacationer who returns to a beloved summer house year after year, the addicted reader opens book three or four or eleven in a given series and is thoroughly at home in the locale — its by now familiar native characters, the verbal shrubbery and the narrative floorboards that occasionally creak.[20]

The sales figures for the Stratemeyer mystery series no longer seem mystifying when we add to all the homely and comfortable seductions mentioned above the opposing appeal of the unknown secret in need of unraveling that is at the heart of the mystery. And this act of balancing predictable formulas with what series promoters called "many strange and dangerous adventures . . . packed with action, suspense and mystery" begs further exploration. Read on, dear readers, to discover *The Secret of the Stratemeyer Syndicate*.

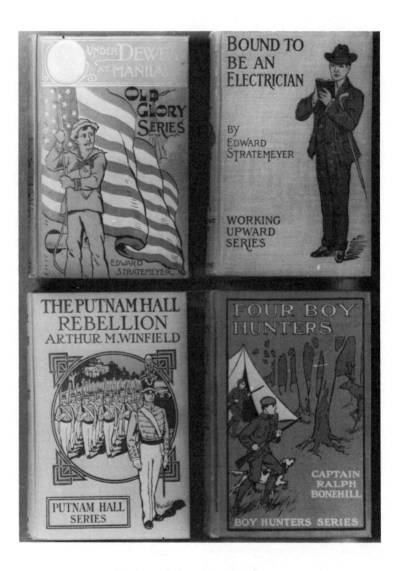

Four of Edward Stratemeyer's own series.

(Sources: *Under Dewey at Manila*, Edward Stratemeyer, Lee and Shepard, 1898; *Bound to Be an Electrician*, Edward Stratemeyer, Allison, 1897; *The Putnam Hall Rebellion*, Arthur M. Winfield, Grosset and Dunlap, 1909; *Four Boy Hunters*, Captain Ralph Bonehill, Cupples and Leon, 1906.)

2

EDWARD STRATEMEYER
The Man and the
Literary Machine

*As a boy . . . . I had quite a library, including many of Optic's and Alger's books.
At seven or eight when I was reading them I said: "If I could only write books
like that I'd be the happiest person on earth."*
— Edward Stratemeyer, *Newark Evening News*, June 4, 1927

Edward Stratemeyer, looking back over his life of sixty-four
years, "edited" in the passage above a moment from his childhood
to bring it neatly into place with the life that followed. This
tendency to revise can be easily explained. A life spent devising
and editing stories whose pieces always fell into place perfectly
would have made it only natural to recast his own life into a
balanced story in which beginnings and endings are harmonious,
and what is more Stratemeyer's life *was* the stuff of the American
dream. He was not the only one to regard it as myth. An article
published in *Fortune* magazine four years after his death called
the man a "Homeric scribe" and his characters "Olympians" and
went on to this aggrandizement regarding the million-dollar estate
he left:

> That was his reward for discovering in the late nineties that,
> like many another natural resource of the time, the reading
> capacity of the American adolescent was limitless. As oil had
> its Rockefeller, literature had its Stratemeyer.[1]

Nearly half a century later, an enthusiastic essayist would claim,

17

"If anyone ever deserved a bronze statue in Central Park, somewhere between Hans Christian Andersen and Alice in Wonderland, it is Edward Stratemeyer, incomparable king of juveniles."[2]

In their retelling, the lives of mythicized figures tend to fall into anecdotal moments that signify the special qualities of the person in question. So one finds in published biographies spurious accounts about George Washington and the cherry tree, Abe Lincoln and the borrowed book he placed in a chink of the log cabin to keep dry. This work is not intended to perpetuate the tradition of raising Stratemeyer's life to the level of hagiography by comparison with these worthies, but his story certainly is one that proceeds by embellished anecdotes such as the item about the prescient youth that appeared in the *Newark Evening News*.

Item number 2. "The Episode of the Brown Wrapping Paper." According to this often retold tale, the twenty-five-year-old Stratemeyer was working at his brother's tobacco store in Elizabeth, New Jersey, one day, and in an off moment he scribbled down a story (of eighteen thousand words) on a good-sized length of brown wrapping paper. Later he sent that story, "Victor Horton's Idea," to *Golden Days* and received by return mail a check for $75, about six times the average weekly wage then. It was published in the Philadelphia-based boys' magazine in 1889, and Stratemeyer's writing career was off and running.

Item number 3. "On the Spot with *Under Dewey at Manila*." Nine years after the brown wrapping paper story was published, Stratemeyer happened to send a book-length manuscript, a war tale, to Lee and Shepard in Boston. The year 1898 also happened to be the date of Commodore Dewey's victory at Manila Bay, and an editor at Lee and Shepard suggested a revision that converted Stratemeyer's war novel into a book about the Spanish-American War. Stratemeyer acquiesced, and a best seller was born, *Under Dewey at Manila; or, The War Fortunes of a Castaway*, as well as the Old Glory series of which it was the first title.

Item number 4. "The Etymology of a Stratemeyer Pseudonym." One of the first pen names used by Edward Stratemeyer was Arthur M. Winfield, under which he published both his Rover Boys series and Putnam Hall series, among others. His obituary in the *New York Times* offered the writer's explanation of the pseudonym: "Arthur" was a near homonym with *author*, "M." stood for the million copies of his books he hoped to see published, and "Winfield" referred to the success he wanted in his chosen profession.[3] Like Babe Ruth's legendary pointing beyond the outfield when he stepped up to bat, Stratemeyer's assumption of "Arthur M. Winfield" was a classic hero's boast before battle. And he lived up to his claims.

As these last three items indicate, Stratemeyer's life, like many of his books, followed the rise-to-respectability pattern set forth in Horatio Alger's novels he so admired as a child. Alger's heroes are forthright, confident, and — above all — industrious and lucky. Stratemeyer, clearly, was composed of goodly measures of these attributes. The other scanty facts available regarding his biography confirm the connection. He was born of German immigrant parents in 1862 in Elizabeth, New Jersey, and attained an eighth-grade education, above average for the period but not the prep-school upbringing many of his characters were to receive. He took a job as a clerk in his brother's tobacco shop and later opened his own stationery store in Newark. All the while he was writing stories for boys' magazines. In 1892, the year after his marriage, he sold fourteen dime novels and five magazine stories, and his first child, a daughter Harriet, was born.

Stratemeyer's luck was demonstrated by his good fortune in attaining a job at the dime novel and magazine publishing house, Street and Smith, where he encountered his childhood heroes, William T. Adams ("Oliver Optic") and Horatio Alger, Jr. On the scene when they died, he was assigned to finish their incomplete manuscripts. At Street and Smith, he also worked beside Upton Sinclair, Gilbert Patten (author of the Frank and Dick Merriwell stories under the name of Burt L. Standish), and Frederic Van Rensselaer Dey, dime novelist extraordinaire and a primary writer of the Nick Carter stories. Stratemeyer contributed to this series, too, between the years 1892 and 1895.

Then there was the lucky coincidence of Dewey's attack and Stratemeyer's war novel for boys. The Midas touch continued to obtain in his literary endeavors throughout the first decade of the twentieth century. It was during this period that he completed from notes — or in some cases, completely invented — eleven volumes attributed to Alger and published posthumously;[4] he also formed his literary syndicate. The rest is history . . . the Rover Boys, Tom Swift, Ruth Fielding, Baseball Joe, Bomba the Jungle Boy, the Hardy Boys, Nancy Drew, Kay Tracey, and on and on. In the end Stratemeyer's bibliography came to some two hundred books actually written by him and an estimated eight hundred others that he outlined and edited.

Good fortune did not spoil Stratemeyer or change his habits. While his office was in Manhattan, he maintained a conservative family life in Newark with his wife and two daughters, keeping membership in the Roseville Athletic Association (where he bowled) and his avid interest in baseball and motoring. And he worked unrelentingly. According to his obituary, he was at his office every working day, usually dictating stories, until pneumonia confined him to bed one week before his death.

Over and above his luck and his industry, there was finally Stratemeyer's amazing resourcefulness, apparent from the start of his career, when it came to knowing what the young reading public wanted and knowing how to manufacture and market the answers to that question: "With the rib of Deadwood Dick and the soul of Tom the Bootblack, he fashioned middle-class Richard Rover who made money for himself, his creator, and his publisher."[5] Stratemeyer's virtually unerring sense of public taste, his business acumen, and his genius in the realm of literary formulas combined to make his characters the ones most admired by American youth of the new century—and the ones most detested by adult guardians of the young and the nation's literary heritage.

It was obvious to Stratemeyer in the first years of the twentieth century that he had a very good thing going. Major juvenile publishing houses, like Grosset and Dunlap and Cupples and Leon, sought his pen with handsome contract offers. His Rover Boys series had exactly the new look in adventure series that turn-of-the-century readers wanted. In fact, that series about escapades at school and on the road was such a winner that Stratemeyer began writing others of the same ilk: Dave Porter first went to Oak Hall in 1905, the Putnam Hall cadets were created in 1901. Arthur Winfield's introduction to the latter series provides an interesting insight into Stratemeyer's sixth business sense:

This series was started at the request of many boys and girls who had read some volumes of the "Rover Boys' Series," and who wanted to know what had taken place at Putnam Hall previous to the arrival there of the three Rover brothers. When the Rovers came on the scene Putnam Hall had been flourishing for some time and was filled with bright, go-ahead cadets, who had been mixed up in innumerable scrapes, and who had gone through quite a few adventures. My young friends wanted to hear all about these wideawake lads, and for their benefit I started this series.[6]

Other adventure series were also in progress—the Outdoor series, about boys hunting, playing baseball, boating, and touring in their cars; the Deep Sea series, a "rattling ocean yarn" about diver Dave Fearless; and what was to become the longest-running Stratemeyer series of all, the Bobbsey Twins, initiated in 1904.[7]

Stratemeyer put two plans into action that changed the history of American juvenile literature. In 1906 he went to one of his publishers, Cupples and Leon, and proposed that they sell his hardcover series books for fifty cents. (The prices at that time varied and went as high as $1.25 a copy.) The Motor Boys, written under the name of Clarence Young, was the first series to be sold as fifty-centers. The books were an immediate success—a Cupples and Leon advertising blurb claimed the group to be "the biggest and best selling series for boys ever published."[8] They did go through thirty-five printings. Other publishers followed suit, and a new pattern of juvenile bookselling was in effect.

The second brainstorm Stratemeyer had at this time—his literary syndicate—was induced by sheer demand. One man could no longer produce annual additions to all the series he had going, not even the indefatigable Stratemeyer. The Stratemeyer Syndicate was probably established in 1906. The incorporation date is 1910, and by that time its chief had set up an office at 24 West Twenty-fifth Street in Manhattan, the Syndicate's home until after Stratemeyer's death in 1930.[9] The plan was simple: Stratemeyer would design Syndicate offerings and continue writing some of the books as time permitted under his own name, under two established pseudonyms (Winfield and Captain Ralph Bonehill), and under new pen names. Other volumes would be farmed out to hired writers. The first series issued by the Syndicate was the Bobbsey Twins, which was published as the work of Laura Lee Hope, in the final analysis one of the most productive of all Stratemeyer Syndicate noms de plume. (Hope's oeuvre was in fact written by at least six writers;[10] among her other series are Bunny Brown and His Sister Sue, the Outdoor Girls, the Moving Picture Girls, and the Blythe Girls.) Other early series that established the Syndicate as the winner in the field were the Motor Boys, begun in 1906; Dorothy Dale, 1908; Tom Swift, 1910; the Motor Girls, 1910; Baseball Joe, 1912; Dave Dashaway, 1913; the Outdoor Girls, 1913; Ruth Fielding, 1913; the Moving Picture Boys and the Motion Picture Chums, both 1913.

From its inception Stratemeyer held tight rein on his Syndicate. He dreamed up new series and for each volume in a series developed an outline that was then given to the contract writer, who in 1930 was paid between $50 and $250 to turn the outline into a two-hundred-page book. Stories are told about Stratemeyer's careful scheduling of appointments so that no two members of the writing staff met as they came and went with their assignments. Next, he revised and proofread each manuscript. Then the book was sent to a publisher — the Syndicate has had more than three dozen in America alone in the last three-quarters of a century. Further, Stratemeyer's Syndicate, not the author nor the publisher, owned all copyrights. This arrangement in itself accounts for the leadership and longevity of the corporation in the ever-changing publishing business.

If Edward Stratemeyer is not a household name, his writers have been even lesser celebrities, especially because the Syndicate has not encouraged dissemination of information about them to the public. (For the same reason no biography of Stratemeyer has ever been authorized, a fact that surely helps to explain the attention given to the anecdotes that pass for his life story.) But a number of Syndicate writers can be identified, and in many instances they are not without professional accomplishment outside their association with Stratemeyer.

Many were former newspaper men and women, like Stratemeyer's second-in-command, Howard Garis. Garis was a writer who could compete with Stratemeyer in productivity. In house, he produced the Motor Boys and some of the Tom Swift and Baseball Joe series, among other responsibilities for the Syndicate. Outside, he was the author of innumerable Uncle Wiggily tales and scores of series books that he sold directly to publishers.[11] Howard was not the only Garis on Stratemeyer's team; his wife, Lillian, and later his children, Roger and Cleo, worked for it, too. Lillian Garis, also a former newspaper staff member, penned a number of the early Syndicate successes such as the Bobbsey Twins, Dorothy Dale, and the Outdoor Girls. Other writers of note for Stratemeyer during the Syndicate's first three decades of operation were St. George Rathbone, Walter Karig (later book editor of the *Washington Post and Times-Herald*), and Canadian Leslie McFarlane (later drama editor for the Canadian Broadcasting Corporation).[12]

After Stratemeyer's death in 1930, his two daughters, Harriet and Edna, oversaw the running of the firm, despite their father's belief that women did not belong in the office.[13] Harriet Stratemeyer Adams moved the Syndicate office to East Orange, New Jersey, to be nearer to her home and immediately began editing the titles her father had left. This was a tall task since he had only recently inaugurated the Nancy Drew series with the publication of three volumes he himself wrote and the Hardy Boys series was just four years old. What was more, during her father's tenure the Syndicate usually had over two dozen series in progress at any given time. Initially the pace of Syndicate publication did not slacken appreciably under the daughters' management; in 1935, fourteen series were ongoing, including—beyond Nancy Drew and the Hardy Boys—such important ones as the Bobbsey Twins, Don Sturdy, Bomba the Jungle Boy, Tom Swift, and Honey Bunch. And two major new series were introduced during Adams's early years as Syndicate chief, the Dana Girls and Kay Tracey.

Over the next forty years the number of vital series fell sharply: nine were in progress in 1940, four by 1980, five today. But this decline does not tell the true story, for some series' popularity has waxed (Bobbseys, Drew, Hardys)—old titles have been revised, new ones issued regularly, and sales have soared. Other series have also come along: the Happy Hollisters; Tom Swift, Jr.; Honey Bunch and Norman; the Bret King Mystery

Stories; and the Linda Craig series. Harriet Stratemeyer Adams directed the growth of the Syndicate for half a century. Her sister became an inactive partner in 1942, but in 1948 former teacher and newspaperman Andrew Svenson joined the Syndicate as a writer. Svenson was responsible for the Happy Hollisters as well as some of the work done in revising and writing new titles for ongoing series.[14] In 1961 he became Adams's partner, a position he held until his death in 1975. Ten years earlier Nancy Axelrad had joined the Syndicate staff as a writer and editor, and she continues her work at present along with partners Lorraine S. Rickle and Lieselotte Wuenn.[15]

If the writers mentioned are not well known, their pseudonyms in many cases are (or were at one time) famous: Victor Appleton, Margaret Penrose, Helen Louise Thorndyke, Clarence Young, Franklin W. Dixon, Alice B. Emerson, Roy Rockwood, Laura Lee Hope, Carolyn Keene, Jerry West. And so the Syndicate and its publishers would have it. At times the latter have gone so far as to create biographies, or at least partial ones, for their "writers." Regarding Margaret Penrose, "author" of the Motor Girls, a Cupples and Leon promotion said: "No one is better equipped to furnish these tales than Mrs. Penrose, who, besides being an able writer, is an expert automobilist." According to a Henry Altemus publicist, Julia K. Duncan, supposed writer of the Doris Force mystery series of the 1930s, based her stories on events from her own life.

Syndicate pseudonyms are very important not only as a way of keeping real writers in check but also for their lasting power. Writers depart the firm or die off; Laura Lee Hope lives on. And if a "writer" has a particularly successful series to his or her credit, the pseudonym can be used to get a follow-up series off to a good start. Thus, after her immensely popular Ruth Fielding books, Alice B. Emerson introduced the Betty Gordon series for the same reading public. In 1934, Carolyn Keene, just four years after beginning her Nancy Drew series, came up with another series about two similar sleuths, the Dana Girls.

Because of its division of labor Stratemeyer's series book business demanded explicitly stated rules for smooth maintenance of the assembly line: six different writers cannot all tell a story in the

manner of Laura Lee Hope without guidelines. Something of
the Syndicate's modus operandi has been revealed from time to
time. At the series level, for instance, an economical and sensi-
ble procedure has long been firmly in place. Series are first introduced with the issuance of three titles. If these meet with public
approval, more follow, and the set is declared a successful "breed-
er" if it runs through at least seven more volumes.[16] Of course,
some series never take off — the Stratemeyer bibliography has its
share of unpopular offerings (the White Ribbon Boys, a series
about "the great modern movement for temperance," begun in
1915; the Flyaways, an unusual fantasy series, begun in 1925;
or the Tollivers, an adventure series about a black family, begun
in 1967). But Stratemeyer's business know-how often led to re-
birth for his discontinued series; the Up and Doing series, begun
and concluded in 1912, later became volumes 1, 2, and 3 of the
Fairview Boys series with the simple shifting of original titles to
the subtitle slots in the new books.[17] Further, advertisements at
the end of series books, into the 1930s, that is, attempted to woo
readers of an already established series to a new and similar one.
And within the books, Stratemeyer, his writers, and some of his
successors religiously employed a convention that could be called
the pearl necklace. No title stands alone, all have their place in
the great series chain. At the outset, in the second chapter as a
rule, previous volumes in the series are plugged, while in the last
pages of the book the next pearl in the series necklace is alluded
to. Over time the initial endorsements have shrunk from substantial exposition about the series, its characters, and their previous
exploits to quick mention of the previous title . . . but the ploy
remains the same.

A noteworthy aspect of the assemblage of a Stratemeyer series
book is its production time. Forty days from conception to the
typeset product was one estimate.[18] (Incidentally, in the start-
up days of the Syndicate, Stratemeyer owned the electrotype plates
and merely leased them to a publisher.) It is reputed that Stratemeyer could write a book in two days, if pressed; Harriet Stratemeyer Adams said she typically completed a mystery in two
months, though she could write one in two weeks.[19] Both faithfully maintained a nine-to-five schedule, the goal each day being
the dictation of three chapters, or seventy-five hundred words.

One Stratemeyer writer, Albert Svenson, has made public his work methods. He replaced the stenographer with the "sound-scriber," a gadget worthy of Tom Swift.[20] Concerning this means of oral composition, and the dictation process in general, Svenson said: "It helps to make dialog jump." My strongest impression upon listening to a Svenson soundscription and then looking at corresponding drafts, galleys, and final printed version of one of his Happy Hollister books was amazement at the small number of changes made throughout the process. Of course, there was a fair amount of structural rearrangement to make the plot flow more smoothly. But beyond that, the alterations were stylistic, trivial, and not all that common — e.g., "fortune hunter" became "treasure hunter"; a weak verb was replaced by a more active one ("'Don't let him fool you,' said Joey wisely" was amended to ". . . , Joey warned"). These preliminary and final versions of *The Happy Hollisters and the Mystery of the Mexican Idol* certainly suggest a writer who knew well the special conventions of story-telling he was to follow. In short, the Stratemeyer fold could work quickly and anonymously because they knew exactly what was expected of them.

Whoever was doing the writing — Syndicate management or contract writers — there was a set procedure. First, a three-page outline was produced. This outline contained such items as a list of the dramatis personae, their fates in the course of the volume, a blow-by-blow plot outline, and the time elements for the novel. And then the writer got to work applying the predictable flesh. There were, no doubt, other understood house guidelines from which writers operated. Svenson once explained that "whether we do yarns about *Übermenschen* or pigtailed Philo Vances, we subscribe to the Stratemeyer formula . . . laid down by old Edward." He went on to lay it out thus:

> A low death rate but plenty of plot. Verbs of action, and polka-dotted with exclamation points and provocative questions. No use of guns by the hero. No smooching. The main character introduced on page one and a slambang mystery or peril set up. Page one used to be fifteen lines, and now it's eighteen.[21]

Elsewhere, Svenson put it succinctly: "The trick in writing children's books is to set up danger, mystery, and excitement on page one. Force the kid to turn the page."[22] And, within the chapter, he explained, there must be a dramatic moment in the plot and at the end a cliff-hanger, whereby the kid is forced another time to turn the page.

As these dicta regarding style, structure, and content make clear, there is a sameness to the Stratemeyer series books that overrides the accommodations that have been made in the last eighty years to a changing American society and transcends, too, the variety of popular literary genres — school/sports story, western, mystery, science fantasy, and others — the Syndicate has worked in. Particular formulas and cultural myths incorporated into Stratemeyer's most popular mystery and suspense series will be scrutinized in later chapters. Here will be mentioned the features of plot, characterization, setting, and style that are the common demoninators of all the series and that have throughout the Syndicate's history brought on attacks by Stratemeyer's myriad detractors.

"Plenty of plot," Svenson said. Stratemeyer's series books depend on action galore, most of it more or less loosely plotted around a conflict between good and bad characters: traps are set, assaults are made on enemy quarters, and chases (in every mode of transportation imaginable) are conducted by the heroes. Their opponents, in turn, spy on, harrass, trick, and sometimes kidnap (but never kill, as Svenson notes) them.[23] It is only natural that out of such suspenseful back-and-forth action the mystery plot would eventually emerge to hold together the thrilling individual episodes. Even in Stratemeyer's own very early work one finds the basic subject of the mystery — the suspenseful uncovering of secrets — underlying all the random adventure. As far back as *Nelson the Newsboy*, an Alger novel finished by Stratemeyer, the newsboy hero must chase down the bully whom he suspects robbed him, and in the end another secret is uncovered when Nelson learns he is the missing son of rich Mark Horton. But whether the emphasis in the book is on an unfolding mystery or, more simply, a string of retaliatory adventures, the primary characteristic of the plot is exciting and provocative physical activity. Svenson is not 100 percent accurate on the "no smooching" point—Dick Rover and Dora Stanhope kiss at least once before they are married, Ruth Fielding kisses Tom impulsively in *Ruth Fielding at Cameron Hall*, and in later Nancy Drew volumes Ned is permitted to kiss Nancy quickly. This romantic action, however, is almost always secondary, only a brief interlude between action-filled adventures. (When a major character married, as the Syndicate found out after Tom Swift took the plunge in 1929, the popularity of the series promptly waned.[24])

As for plot resolution, there always is a conspicuous one. At the end of every story, the assorted adventurous scenes are neatly synchronized and loose ends tied up, if need be. Then the deeds of the heroes or heroines are heartily acclaimed by friends, relatives, even public officials. And, as in the classic detective tale, vice never pays. It should be pointed out that this theme, the preservation of order by unmasking those trying to topple it through their scheming, is fundamentally conservative. It rewards the "Olympians," as Stratemeyer's protagonists were called in *Fortune* magazine, who already have the advantage by dint of birth, ability, or previous achievement; and it punishes those out to wreak havoc with the status quo by trying to gain what is not their due. Later, Syndicate offerings adapted this plot of good against evil to include political themes being played out in the real world; some of the new and revised series mysteries of the 1960s and 1970s, for example, make the suspenseful action global in scope. The Communists replace more generic low-life or foreign villains as the bad characters working to undermine the all-American heroes risking their all for the free world. Thus, while there is sensational, or at least titillating, action in the Stratemeyer series, the themes embedded in that action are anything but subversive.

Some few of the Stratemeyer series contain action that takes place in locales that can be pinpointed on the map. The second set of Rover Boys, when they aren't in school or on the road, live on Riverside Drive in Manhattan; the Blythe Girls, an interesting series started in 1925 and credited to Laura Lee Hope, go to live and work in Manhattan when their parents die; and Baseball Joe makes it to the Big Leagues and real big-city life after a humble start in a mythical small town. The majority of the series, however, have their home bases in make-believe towns not far from

a major city — towns with names like Lakeport, Bayport, Clare-
mont, Shopton, and River Heights — or in equally insular and
fictitious school settings (Oak Hill, Putnam Hall, Cameron Hall,
Brill College, etc.). And, of course, the more exotic settings in
series like Don Sturdy and Bomba the Jungle Boy are clearly
"otherworldly" realms. Wherever the action is set, the place proves
to be amazingly, unnaturalistically amenable to the doings of the
central characters. Local authorities offer no real resistance and
sometimes are even helpful. Parents, if present, are good-natured
and generally supportive. In short, the milieu makes no demands
on characters, never inhibiting their quests or testing their mettle.
The effect of such made-to-order backdrops for Stratemeyer's
plots is, interestingly, a feeling of timelessness: Karla Kuskin has
called the Hardys' Bayport an "all American Shangri-la."[25]

Leading characters in Stratemeyer's series are, to quote
Svenson once more, *Übermenschen*. They are exaggerated types,
not perfect but indisputably extraordinary adolescents. They are,
for instance, skilled at everything that comes their way, be the
challenge a matter of commerce, science, the arts, or sports. The
typecasting is due, in part, to the writers' meager use of description concerning series stars and also their adamant aversion to
exploring characters' thoughts in any depth. Initially, protagonists
came only in sets: the Boy Hunters, the Outdoor Girls, the
Darewell Chums, the Motor Girls, the Motor Boys. But for a
few superficial physical and temperamental distinctions, the groups
in these series were composed of identical elements. While the
practice of heroes and heroines in the plural never died out, solo
stars began to appear alongside the groups. Tom Swift, Ruth
Fielding, Bomba, Nancy Drew, Kay Tracey, Linda Craig — these
characters may be flanked by assistants and/or well-wishers, but
their achievement is singular, and their supporting cast are only foils that make this point plain. The supporting figures, what
is more, tend to be typed to an even greater extent than the main
characters (the fat friend, usually a clown; the admiring, often
mooning, romantic interest; the good sport; the valiant underdog).

Just as the good characters are superior in all ways, the
wicked ones are bad through and through. The evildoers in the
Stratemeyer series books hold none of the ambiguous fascina-

tion and repulsion of the consummately wicked witches, ogres, and stepmothers in the fairy tales. Stratemeyer's villains are bullies, simpering cowards, or snotty social climbers, and they always recognize these basic truths immediately when confronted by the protagonist(s) at the end of the story. So, while they put up a good fight that keeps the plot moving at breakneck speed, they, too, are ultimately and predictably mere foils for the good characters to triumph over.

The series characters, good and bad, share a recognizable manner of speaking. Some — for example, the groupies of the primary characters — are given to telling obvious and corny jokes. In order to enhance the suspense no doubt, they also utter mild expletives regularly, exclamations ranging from clichés ("Yikes!" or "Holy catfish!" or "Snakes!") to the idiosyncratic: Mr. Damon in the Tom Swift is well known for blessing every imaginable part of his wardrobe, from his hat to his shoelaces. Add to these formulaic habits of speech the equally predictable dialects of the lower-class villains, and black servants in early Stratemeyer series, and questions are raised as to how successfully the dialogue "jumps," in Svenson's word.

Main characters exclaim abundantly, too; but in addition to the sort of gratuitous invocation mentioned above, they are often given to overflowings of feeling, usually at the end of a volume. This is particularly true of the girls' books, where there is a residue of the Pollyanna tradition of gushing. At the close of *Betty Gordon and the Mystery Girl*, for instance, the protagonist rubs her cheek affectionately against her uncle's coat sleeve and says confidentially, "I'm so happy . . . because every one else is happy!"[26] Even as late as 1962 western sleuth Linda Craig oozes "What a wonderful clue!" upon finding mysterious horse tracks in the dust.[27] Moreover, heroes are not above such unctuous remarks as Dick Rover's exclamation in *The Rover Boys Winning a Fortune*, "I'll tell you what — old friends are best! . . . Every one of them is sticking to us like glue!"[28] Or take Harry's declaration in *The Automobile Boys of Lakeport*: "Automobiling can't be beat! . . . It's the best sport yet!"[29] One other verbal tic common to protagonists of both sexes is the tendency to hurl imperatives at their foes, urging them to confess their crime, come out of hiding, or give back whatever they stole.

The real creakiness in the style of many Stratemeyer series books, it must be admitted, is the fault of the omniscient narrator, not the characters in his story. The first Syndicate books are the worst in this regard, no doubt because they were following the laborious example set by Horatio Alger; but, truth compels me to say, the mechanical awkwardness did not fade quickly. In 1916 the narrator of *The Outdoor Girls at Ocean View* announces her presence loudly, "The three girls were laughing and — yes, truth compels me to say they were giggling — when the door of the shop swung open."[30] Such intrusions are most common at the beginnings and conclusions of series novels: "And now let me add a few words more and then bring to an end this story of 'Dave Porter and His Double.'"[31] Another place that lends itself to awkward narration is the requisite summary of earlier titles in chapter 2. In *Battling the Wind*, Ted Scott is caught in a storm and his plane is diving wildly when the narrator steps in:

> And so, while he is watching that awful plunge with the fear of impending death in his heart, it may be well for the benefit of those who have not read the preceding volumes of this series to tell who Ted Scott was, and what his adventures had been up to the time this story opens.[32]

When the series book writer is not making such glaring remarks, his style creaks in other fashions. Sometimes the syntax is unnecessarily stilted: "Vivid and lovely was Rose with the bobbed golden hair and the hat that matched the blue of her eyes."[33] Or, from the Ted Scott novel cited above: "Ted Scott, the greatest aviator of all time, the idol of the American people, turned about in surprise" (p. 34). Then, as the years passed, the house writers developed pet constructions that they used over and over again. The "Tom Swiftie" — "Tom said soothingly," "Tom said questioningly," and so on — is famous, and it is by no means confined to Victor Appleton's prose.[34] There is another favored usage that is even more pervasive in the Stratemeyer series: the introductory participial phrase. It could be dubbed the "Nancy Drewster," since it appears most noticeably in Carolyn Keene's writing. Here are a few examples taken from the 1959 revision of the first title in the series, *The Secret of the Old Clock*:

Becomingly dressed in a tan cotton suit, Nancy set off in her convertible for the shopping district.[35]

Acting on an impulse, Nancy sprinted to her car. (p. 127)

Reaching the car, Nancy sprang inside. (p. 133)

Focusing her flashlight, she peered hopefully into the dark interior. (p. 128)

These prescriptive literary formulas force doubts as to the accuracy of the first part of this advertisement for a 1931 Stratemeyer series, Doris Force: "With a keen sense of humor, and delicate weaving of character, she [Julia Duncan] unfolds her plot with adventurous action in every chapter." And literary quality is one of the grounds on which the Stratemeyer Syndicate has been publicly attacked throughout its eighty-year history; librarians, educators, and literary critics have long lamented the literary inadequacies of the Stratemeyer publications. An editorial in the December 1905 issue of *Library Journal*, for example, specifically questioned the aesthetic merit of early Stratemeyer series: "Shall the libraries resist the flood and stand for a better and purer literature and art for children, or shall they 'meet the demands of the people' by gratifying a low and lowering taste [for the series]?"[36]

But the fundamental objections of the many adults who have deplored the Stratemeyer corpus usually concern other matters, like the assembly-line method of mass producing the series thrillers. The most frequently voiced complaint of all (and it has been voiced for over half a century now) is that these books are "sensationalist," "trashy," "vulgar," "cheap," and "tawdry" — in short, anything but what publicists claimed for one Stratemeyer girls' series, the Outdoor Girls: "These are the tales of the various adventures participated in by a group of bright, fun-loving girls. . . . They are clean and wholesome and free from sensationalism." This "sensationalist" argument emphasized not so much the method of production but the dangers of consumption that lurk in what Franklin K. Mathiews, Chief Scout Librarian of the Boy Scouts of America, called racy, "mile-a-minute" fiction. In other words, adults perceived and resented the hold Stratemeyer's suspenseful formula fiction had on young readers.

The ranting was the loudest in the first two decades of this century when Mathiews and James E. West, the chief executive of the Boy Scouts, mounted their name-calling campaign against series fiction — especially Stratemeyer's. In an amazing article that one-ups Stratemeyer on the sensationalist score, "Blowing Out the Boy's Brains," Mathiews links the new "underground library" (the series books) with the earlier and pernicious dime novel. And he accuses these new books of crippling boys' imaginations by their excessiveness:

> Because these cheap books do not develop criminals or lead boys, except very occasionally, to seek the Wild West, parents who buy such books think they do their boys no harm. The fact is, however, that the harm done is simply incalculable. I wish I could label each one of these books: "Explosives! Guaranteed to Blow Your Boy's Brains Out." . . . The red-blooded boy, the boy in his early teens, must have his thrill; he craves excitement, has a passion for action, "something must be doing" all the time; and in nothing is this more true than in his reading. . . .
>
> [In the series book] no effort is made to confine or control these highly explosive elements. The result is that, as some boys read such books, their imaginations are literally "blown out," and they go into life as terribly crippled as though by some material explosion they had lost a hand or foot. . . . Why are there so few men readers of the really good books . . . ? Largely, I think, because the imagination of so many men as boys received such brutal treatment at the hands of those authors and publishers who give no concern as to what they write or publish so long as it returns constantly the expected financial gain.[37]

Earlier in his fulminations Mathiews objected to the fact that in the series books "insuperable difficulties and crushing circumstances are as easily overcome and conquered as in fairy tales," and it is an interesting coincidence that a very similar battle had been waged some one hundred years before by those opposing sensationalism in the fairy tales, which were then being given anew to the young. Mrs. Sarah Trimmer had preached:

We doubt not but that many besides ourselves can recollect, their horrors of imagination on reading *Blue Beard*. . . . A moment's consideration will surely be sufficient to convince people of the least reflection, of the danger, as well as the impropriety, of putting such books as these [*Cinderella* and *Little Red Riding Hood* as well as *Blue Beard*] into the hands of little children, whose minds are susceptible of every impression; and who from the liveliness of their imaginations are apt to convert into realities whatever forcibly strikes their fancy.[38]

In the 1960s and 1970s librarians and critics could still be heard to utter, in more muted tones as a rule, complaints not unlike Mathiews. Selma Lanes, for example, names Stratemeyer's best-selling series "escapist," "wooden," "regressive."[39] But today ongoing series are issued in "library editions," and most librarians have given in and put Stratemeyer on their shelves, arguing contra Mathiews that they just may hook a child on reading fiction and then reading *other* fiction. In between the present and Mathiews' criticism, there have also appeared a sizeable number of studies regarding the actual popularity of the series books with young readers. While it was the intention of the writers of these reports to warn parents and others of the extent to which the series thriller had insinuated itself in young society, they also provided statistical documentation as to just how successful Stratemeyer and others were in finding an audience.[40]

It is indeed ironic that these series books, in so many ways bastions of conservative middle-class thinking about social issues, should be deemed "explosive" because of their superficial action. But for the majority of American boys and girls between the ages of seven and thirteen, the hue and cry of well-meaning adults has mattered not a whit. The literary inferiority of Stratemeyer's fiction is not a concern to them; in fact, it may be a comforting "plus." And as for the escapist or unrealistic aspect of the novels, the young have always shown a predilection for fantasy; and Stratemeyer's coupling of fantastical adventure with "up-to-date" characters and scenery only serves to encourage readers' interest.

Probably the adult outcry even abetted the mysterious or adventurous aspect of reading these books — it added to the potent internal appeals of the books the external attraction of their being forbidden fruit. Many a Stratemeyer title has been devoured on the sly or undercover, maybe literally under the covers by flashlight after hours or behind the added cover of a suitably respectable dust jacket. In L. M. Montgomery's *Anne of Green Gables*, a precursor of Stratemeyer girls' series, the titular heroine, aged 13 3/4, confesses:

> Miss Stacy . . . found me reading a book one day called, *The Lurid Mystery of the Haunted Hall*. . . . and, oh Marilla, it was so fascinating and creepy. It just curdled the blood in my veins. But Miss Stacy said it was a very silly, unwholesome book, and she asked me not to read any more like it, but it was *agonizing* to give back that book without knowing how it turned out.[41]

Anne may well have sneaked back to such books later, in part because secret reading is fun in and of itself. Likewise, Stratemeyer's legacy — respectable or not — is read on, night after night, reader after reader, generation after generation.

"You'll tell all you know without the dollar!"
cried Dick.

—*The Rover Boys Down East*
Arthur M. Winfield
Grosset and Dunlap, 1911

3

THE ROVER BOYS
Suspense at School and on the Road

"We owe you and the others a great deal."
"All of you are regular heroes!"
"Heroes? Pooh!" sniffed Tom. "Nothing of the sort. We are just wide-awake American boys."
And they are wide-awake; aren't they, kind reader?
— *The Rover Boys on the River*

Edward Stratemeyer wrote and published his Rover Boys series from 1899–1926 under the name of Arthur M. Winfield. Of the thirty-volume output, the first twenty — that is, those appearing through 1916 — concern the first generation of Rovers: Dick, Tom, and Sam. Their four sons are the subjects of the final ten volumes, called the "Second Rover Boys Series." Indeed, there was another spinoff series, the Putnam Hall Cadets, which chronicles the adventures of the students who preceded the first generation of Rovers at the military academy mentioned in the series title. An early effort in the series book market, the Rover Boys line has nonetheless held its own on publishers' sales charts: among contemporary Stratemeyer books, only the Bobbsey Twins and Tom Swift outsold the Rovers, and the series continued to sell well until mid-century.

Writing in the *Atlantic Monthly* in 1900, Everett T. Tomlinson remarked that "the story of American school life has not yet been written."[1] Not surprisingly, he disdained the Rovers, who were, in fact, among several turn-of-the-century American cousins of the protagonist in the English *Tom Brown's Schooldays*.[2] The three Rovers first enroll at Putnam Hall and later at Brill College; their sons, in turn, are students at Colby Hall, an academy run by a former schoolmate of their fathers. At least half a dozen of the thirty titles in the two series concentrate on school days and their attendant boyish adventures, games, and hijinks. But the fact remains that many more of the books begin where school leaves off. The Rover Boys—all seven of them—are given to daydreaming even when school is in session (particularly at exam time) about how they will spend their upcoming vacation. As Sam reminds his two brothers *in January* in *The Rover Boys at College*, "Remember summer will soon be here . . . and then we can go on a dandy trip somewhere."[3]

The Rover Boys live up to their name. They travel and run up against adventure over much of the western hemisphere, as a quick survey of early titles in the series suggests: *The Rover Boys on the Ocean, or, A Chase for Fortune*; *The Rover Boys in the Jungle, or, Stirring Adventures in Africa*; *The Rover Boys Out West, or, The Search for a Lost Mine*; *The Rover Boys on the Great Lakes, or, The Secret of the Island Cave*. Their sons as well spend more time out of school than in—on a hunt, at Big Horn Ranch, shipwrecked, on Sunset Trail. The adventures enjoyed by the Rover Boys are many and varied. At the most trivial, their suitcases are repeatedly stolen, the tires of their vehicles are caused to blow out, fake telegrams are sent in their names. More significantly, they track down stolen mortgage money; Tom Rover is once accused of stealing ten thousand dollars from a lady on a train; they have their houseboat stolen (with their girlfriends aboard); they pursue Wall Street thieves; and, most often of all, they search for treasure, which as a rule is hidden on islands.

Some of the books, it is true, remain at the level of random adventurous escapades, but as the series evolved, these adventures were commonly organized into larger patterns of suspense. In the best of the stories suspense results from the Rovers' uncovering of some deeper scheme, which has been elaborately premeditated by a set of villains whose main motivation in life appears to be their desire to do in the Rover Boys. The series thus becomes the successor, among boy readers, to Sherlock Holmes and especially Nick Carter, the clever and virtuous sleuth who bridged the gap between the dime novels read by boys in the nineteenth century and the series books they turned to at the beginning of the twentieth.[4]

In 1901 an anonymous reviewer for *St. Nicholas*, the premier periodical for American children, argued:

> Reading only highly spiced stories of adventure, heroism, or mystery, and accounts of strange circumstances that could arise perhaps once in a thousand lives, tends to give wrong ideas of life and of the people we meet every day. The quiet man who sits in the dark corner of the railway-car, with his hat pulled over his brows, and wearing green or blue spectacles, is much more likely to be an invalid with weak eyes than a mysterious detective. If you spend a summer by the sea, the chances of your finding Captain Kidd's treasure are hardly worth considering; and should you dig for it, you would be likely to waste much time that might be devoted to good fun, sensible exercise, or the study of sea-animals or -plants.[5]

Such a magazine as *St. Nicholas* would not deign to publish reviews of series books or mention them by name in their regular "Books and Reading for Young Folk" department — nowhere in the review cited does the writer name the Rover Boys or Edward Stratemeyer (or Arthur M. Winfield). But he might as well have, for his description fits perfectly. Of course, it made no real difference, one way or the other, because the reviewer was whistling in the wind. For the next half century, and beyond, boys and girls were to thrive on just the sort of mystery and adventure stories he maligned.

Winfield's style provides reason enough to ban his books from the review pages of respectable magazines. The writing in the Rover Boys series is the verbal equivalent of a maiden aunt's parlor, full of predictably overstuffed chairs and lace antimicassars. "Fancy prose and polysyllabic thrills," one critic has termed it.[6] The Rovers and their young ladies (continually described as "blushing") do not write letters: they exchange tender epistles. Boys are never just boys in the series; rather, lads develop a propensity for fun. Instead of saying "the group arrived by Mississippi riverboat yesterday," the author writes, "the party to which they belonged had reached the town on their journey down the Father of Waters the day before."[7] Further, the dialect spoken by the minor characters in the series not only smacks of stereotypical notions regarding race, ethnic origin, and social class, but it is hackneyed in the extreme. Alexander Pop's shuffling black servant's speech, the German students' thick dialect and thick-headed responses, the rustic Mr. Sanderson's language of the rube — all are so conventional as to be parodic, the stuff of vaudeville. Fredric Jameson has observed about the language of Raymond Chandler's characters: "clichés and stereotyped speech patterns are heated into life by the presence behind them of a certain form of emotion, that which you would feel in your dealings with strangers."[8] In the Rover Boys books the stereotyped dialogue is not heated, but frozen.

Wide reading in the Rovers tempts one to conclude that Stratemeyer was a little self-conscious in his role of celebrated author to an increasing readership of American boys. Winfield's formal letters of introduction at the beginning of each title hint at the writer's intense concern over establishing a relationship with his audience — and interest in making sure his readers have their bearings before they begin the tale. Or maybe Stratemeyer simply enjoyed assuming the mantle of avuncular and authoritative storyteller, for he surely exaggerates that stance time and again within the novels.

Sometimes Winfield's intrusion into the tale he tells serves to create suspense, as in *Southern Waters* when he enters at chapter's end to allude to the upcoming adventure: "None of them dreamed of what that night was to bring forth" (p. 40). Here, foreshadowing works like the conventional cliff-hanging ending: both — through either prediction or predicament — force the reader to turn the page. More often, the author lolls self-indulgently in his role as unraveler of the tale *to no effect*. As late as 1925, in the penultimate book of the second series, Winfield hangs on to old ways. Randy Rover has just narrowly escaped drowning, and the narrator steps in and drowns out all emotion and excitement: "And now I think it's high time that I pause for a moment to introduce the Rover Boys and their friends to those who are meeting them for the first time."[9] In subsequent series published by the Stratemeyer Syndicate, such narrative "decorations" dwindled appreciably so that the style, while remaining predictable, was brisker. But the Rover Boys, Stratemeyer's first great hit, shows the extent to which he straddled two traditions. His laborious style in these books is but one indicator that he looks back to the formality of nineteenth-century writers for the young as surely as he ushers in a new era in popular adventure literature.

The ornamentations of the author's style notwithstanding, the Rover Boys books are suspenseful "reads." Young readers are capable of reading right through all manner of surface-level obfuscation to find a good story, as the one-time popularity among the young of *Pilgrim's Progress* or *Gulliver's Travels* demonstrates. What exactly are the thrills awaiting the consumer of the Rover Boys volumes? A summary of a representative title in the series, *The Rover Boys Down East*, provides a starting place from which to answer that question.

In this story the three Rovers — Dick, Tom, and Sam — are students at Brill College, elsewhere in the series described as a small midwestern institution on a par with Yale or Princeton. The first chapter opens with a baseball game being played by two teams made up of Brill collegians. On the fifth page of the novel Arthur M. Winfield presents a blow-by-blow account of the progression of the series to date, starting at the very beginning when the boys were cadets at Putnam Hall. The history of the romance between Dick Rover and Dora Stanhope is related — they are now engaged — as are those between Tom and Dora's cousin Nellie Laning and Sam and Nellie's sister Grace. The three girls are conveniently students at Hope Seminary, located less than two miles from Brill. The final section of Winfield's long exposition contains a listing of the Rovers' classmates and acquaintances, the bullies and rascals along with the heroes' special friends.

In short, *The Rover Boys Down East* gets off to a tedious start, but one that is not without promise of a thickening plot. One of the adversaries, Tad Sobber, who was thought dead, is still alive. The voice of the author rings out the chapter with this revelation: "Tad Sobber was to cause a great deal of trouble, as we shall learn in the near future."[10]

The action picks up at once. Chapter 2 concerns a fire on

board the *Thistle*, a boat being used to transport the girls from Hope to their picnic. The Rovers come to the rescue, and there is occasion for Dora to introduce the first real complication in the plot. Josiah Crabtree ("the person mentioned will be remembered by my old readers," Winfield notes) exercises a hypnotic influence on Mrs. Stanhope and has all but forced a marriage, as a way of securing her fortune.

At this point, the tale turns to immediate happenings at school. The boys study for term exams, and there is considerable bantering among them and their friends.

Next the narrative follows not Crabtree, nor Sobber and his uncle Sid Merrick — the three vilest characters in the book — but their lower-level lackeys: Dudd Flockley and two other former students at Brill, Jerry Koswell and Bart Larkspur. The last two have returned to campus and seem to be plotting something, luring the weak Flockley into their schemes.

Winfield resumes the innocuous tale of school tomfoolery, which reveals the character and temperament of the three heroes. They are not goody-goodies, we learn when they set off fireworks without permission. The Rovers, particularly Tom, have a penchant for firecrackers throughout the series; here they ignite the coat of crochety old Professor Asa Sharp but in the end are in no way censured.

Next the boys take the train to the home of Aunt Martha and Uncle Randolph in Cedarville (New York, presumably). When the boys aren't at school or off on adventures, their aunt and uncle's farm is their domicile, as it is for their father, Anderson Rover, a frequently convalescing mineral expert, goldmine proprietor, traveler, and Wall Street financier. Winfield devotes attention to events surrounding the boys' homecoming and then to the Fourth of July party they hold for the girls and Dora's mother, replete with fireworks. There is at last a development in the suspense plot, for the holiday gathering affords Mrs. Stanhope the opportunity to ask Mr. Rover to invest her fortune for her — and Tad Sobber, eavesdropping from nearby bushes, overhears this conversation about the money he claims is rightfully his.

Eleven chapters into the book, the school and domestic merriment is once and for all replaced by adventures on land and

sea. First, the boys are off to camp on Lake Nasco. But rain
dampens that outing, and dad's telegram that he has not received
Mrs. Stanhope's money, which she supposedly sent, brings the
boys rushing back to Cedarville. It is noteworthy that while they
were to this point by and large in the dark as to the machinations of their enemies, the Rovers, once brought into the investigation of the mysterious disappearance of the Stanhope fortune, become infallible sleuths.

Dora is distraught when her mother disappears along with
the money, but Dick tells her to leave the mystery solving to the
boys. Immediately the three go on the trail of the swindlers, a
chase that takes them up the east coast and out onto the islands
of Casco Bay in Maine. Throughout this caper, they run into
more than their fair share of cooperative tramps and witnesses,
one of whom just happened to see a car speeding toward Albany
carrying a woman who shouted "Boston" as she went by.

The freedom of the open road and the thrill of the chase
more than make up for these weaknesses in the mystery plot. The
boys are off with their father's blessing: "Run them down if you
possibly can. Do not spare expense" (p. 189). They borrow a
friend's "dandy" car, suffering in time the inevitable blowout.
They find an important clue, Mrs. Stanhope's handkerchief
(luckily it was initialed!), and then shift from land to water
transportation:

> The Rover Boys were accustomed to quick action, and they
> had supplied themselves with plenty of ready cash to use in case
> of emergency. Consequently, it was an easy matter for them
> to pick up a steam tug at one of the docks. (p. 216)

The captain of the boat is ready to lend them pistols, but
instead they give him a hundred dollars as an inducement to find
Mrs. Stanhope. Out on Casco Bay, following a tip, they maneu-
ver through all the summer pleasure boats and head directly for
the isle of Chesoque, the perfect outpost for their enemies since
it is known to be used by smugglers and to be inhabited by
numerous snakes. (Crabtree was earlier described as "belong[ing]
to the snake-in-the-grass variety of rascals.") When the Rovers
reach the island, they take the precaution of arming themselves,

a good thing because the collection of foes on the island — Koswell, Larkspur, Crabtree, and all the rest — have guns.

Dick eventually becomes a prisoner of the enemy and even though badly bruised (the pistols remain props in most Rover Boys books) immediately challenges Tad Sobber, "What have you done with Mrs. Stanhope?" (p. 259). Later, he aggressively asks Crabtree about his sudden marriage to Mrs. Stanhope; and the man is so taken aback that he stammers and confesses that they are only "as good as married." In other words, the Rovers are in time to save both the woman and the fortune. There is a climactic brawl, after which Mrs. Stanhope is rescued from the waters of the bay. She leads them to the loot in the cave, and then they all go home to Cedarville. The boys receive the praises of their girlfriends and everybody else concerned.

This particular plot nicely represents the hybrid quality of the Rover Boys series; perhaps it is worth mentioning that this title occupies a middle position in the series — it was the fifteenth volume. *The Rover Boys Down East* is, at once, a school story, a travel adventure, a mystery, and even a love story. The last element would seem an unlikely occurrence in boys' fiction, for affairs of the heart have historically combined with mysteries consumed primarily by women and girls, but rarely with those read by men and boys. Nonetheless, the Rover Boys series throughout is genuinely concerned with matters of courtship, marriage, and offspring. In its course all three Rover Boys, in lockstep progression, marry the girls they met back in their Putnam Hall days, establish (adjacent) residences in New York City, become responsible men of business, and have children who, in turn, are packed off to school and develop their own definite romantic interests. In other words, the females in the Rover Boys books are not mere frills, as they are in later Stratemeyer Syndicate mysteries for boys and in much American detective fiction geared for adult male readers. Intrigues of a romantic nature provide actual subplots in a number of volumes. Competing suitors are usually the issue, though in *Down East* Dick is involved in protecting his fiancée's family fortune. And the ritual events of personal romance — namely, proposals, engagement announcements, and weddings — are given much space and weight in the scheme of these stories.[11]

While important ingredients, the school and dating games in *Down East* and the series as a whole are clearly secondary to suspenseful adventure and mystery. On this front Winfield favors melodramatic heightening of episode and conflict. The Rover Boys do not simply encounter excitement; it is perpetrated on them by a ring of opposition that extends far and wide, including classmates, former teachers who have become hardened criminals, and veteran shysters and hoodlums who, you would think, would find tormenting the Rovers decidedly small change. Further, as the first three Rover Boys are followed by their sons, so some of the adversaries produce children bent on thwarting the heroes. The Rovers do indeed have cause to be paranoid, and they are—especially Tom, who when acute depression comes over him (only for a time, of course), asks: "What's the use of keeping in the grind day after day, like a horse on a tread mill? . . . They are all against me, every one of 'em."[12]

The network of opposition to the Rovers is introduced at the outset of the series. Josiah Crabtree appears in the first title, *The Rover Boys at School*, as do Arnold and his son Dan Baxter. Crabtree and Dan Baxter can be counted on to be lurking around the next corner in much of the remainder of the series. In *The Rover Boys on Land and Sea*, for example, the three Rovers travel across the continent during an unexpected school vacation; and as soon as they arrive in San Francisco, they catch a glimpse of Baxter disappearing around a hotel corner. (Baxter, by the way, does make a brief appearance in *Down East*, though he is by no means a central foe in that book.) Though they get even with those out to get them by the end of each novel, the boys are initially at a disadvantage, as in *Down East*, where they begin with little information regarding the efforts being made to seduce Mrs. Stanhope and gain her wealth.

The pitch and the pace of Winfield's narratives also partake of the melodramatic, or the hyperbolic. Pitch refers to noise level. These are very loud books, full of firecrackers popping, tires blowing out, cannons being fired, and—occasionally—a few random gunshots. All this clamor escalates and sustains the excitement caused by the action, even though it is presented in Winfield's stuffy and sobering style. "A loud report came from one of the rear tires," is hardly a lively announcement of a blowout.

Pacing, on the other hand, is something Winfield excels at. In *Down East* he more than makes up for the attenuated beginning in later chapters, where Franklin K. Mathiews' description, "mile-a-minute fiction," is most apt.[13] The Rover Boys are constantly in motion in the second half of the book, the pace reminiscent of a Keystone Cops film. The number of telegrams sent, and intercepted, in the typical Rovers story augments the already considerable amount of activity. Not only are the boys on the go, but so are their foes, as the frenetic pace of the mail points out. The pace of the action increases at the end of most volumes, climaxing in some sort of badly needed cathartic confrontation — a free-for-all fistfight in *Down East*.

It is natural that such heightened adventure would eventually be wedded to the mystery genre in the Rovers series. This union surely occurred elsewhere in the development of detective fiction in America. To stories of the hunt or the chase, which went back to Fenimore Cooper's Leatherstocking and the dime novel western, the mystery was grafted. Emphasis on discovery or detection proved a helpful means of organizing and explaining characters' actions and, more importantly, of synchronizing the various episodes that loosely added up to the adventure story plot. The multiplicity of adventure-filled scenes in *Down East* — at school, at home, and on the road — begs for some kind of integration, and the key mystery plot, involving the investigation of a robbery and a kidnapping, provides just that. It binds together assorted events and brings them to resolution at the end when the stolen goods and the criminals' schemes are uncovered. In its blending of mystery and adventure, the average Rover Boys book is little different from preceding Nick Carter stories, described by A. E. Murch as an "unvarying sequence of crime, flight, pursuit and capture, with physical endurance more important than detective acumen."[14]

The paraphernalia of detection, what is more, contributes a special stature to the events of the novel. Coincidental happenings — for example, Mrs. Stanhope's dropping of her handkerchief — become "direct clews" and thereby take on an importance in the larger plot (and serve to aggrandize the abilities of whoever finds or "reads" these clues). Dick Rover's highly speculative scenario in *Down East* is likewise given extra weight when likened to the workings of a thinking detective:

"It may be that he [Sobber] came here, heard Mrs. Stanhope ask dad to invest the money for her, and heard dad say
that he would let her know when he wanted the cash. Then,
perhaps, he went off, and sent Mrs. Stanhope a bogus letter,
or telegram, signing dad's name."

"Say, Dick, you're a regular sleuth!" cried Fred. "I guess
you've got it straight." (p. 156)

And when Dora reminds Dick that the Cedarville police will be
of no use in a "matter of such importance," Dick concurs and confesses that a couple of first-class detectives have been called in
to help the Rover Boys on the case.

Thus the plot of *Down East*, which follows one of the oldest
and simplest mystery formulas — the treasure hunt — is raised to
the level of an official investigation. Interestingly, the fortune
that the Rovers set out to recover, a tangible end to a search,
recedes in importance as the story progresses. A larger issue —
the discovery of who is secretly plotting against the boys and how
they are going about it — increasingly occupies the heroes' minds.
And since the reader was more knowledgeable about the plot
abroad than the protagonists in the book, he must have fidgeted
nervously (and read on at a pace rivaling the Rovers') when
observing the characters he sided with being spied upon or set
up. Winfield uses dramatic irony most effectively to augment
suspense.

The melodramatic mystery adventure plots that constitute the
main appeal of the Rover Boys books dictate that characterization be handled in broad stripes rather than fine brush strokes
and that characters be known chiefly by their deeds, not their
own or others' reflections. In these stories played out in double
time, not much room exists for hesitation or contemplation. The
presentation of Dick, Tom, and Sam Rover illustrates my point.

The three Rovers are differentiated; the contrasts among
them, in fact, are Winfield's chief means of identifying or describ-
ing the boys. Dick is a typical eldest son. He makes the highest
marks on all school exams; and as we see in *Down East*, where
he is the sleuth who knows exactly what must be done to rescue
Mrs. Stanhope and her money, Dick is the unchallenged leader
of the trio. Elsewhere he is counted on to plan trips, organize

ball games, or arrange outings with the girls. When Anderson
Rover becomes ill, it is Dick who leaves Brill to join — and save —
his father's Wall Street firm. In short, he is characterized as the
initiator of action.

Tom Rover, the exuberant middle son, belongs to the "bad
boy" tradition in American children's books, a character that
emerged after the Civil War but was still evident in the boys'
classic published in 1914, Booth Tarkington's *Penrod*. Like the
rambunctious Penrod, Tom is an adult's picture of a (not so very)
bad boy. All the Rovers are, at bottom, clean-living and cour-
teous: they drink ginger ale at their parties, do not smoke, and
can generally be counted on to conduct themselves decorously.
In *The Rover Boys on Land and Sea*, the girls underline their in-
tegrity in a conversation with the miscreant Baxter:

> "I wouldn't touch liquor if I was starving!" cried Grace.
> "And neither would the Rover Boys," added Dora.
> "Oh, you think the Rover Boys are regular saints!" grum-
> bled the bully. "You don't know what they would do behind
> your back."
> "If they said they wouldn't drink, they wouldn't," cried
> Nellie, her eyes flashing. "We can trust them every time."[15]

Nonetheless, Tom is indeed the prankster of the Rover clan,
always ready with a firecracker or a funny retort in his youth and
even in his young manhood something of a hellion. When he proposes to Nellie in *The Rover Boys in Business*, he admits, "of course,
it is something of a job for a fellow who is full of fun to settle
down."[16] Tom's temper has a short fuse as well; he's quick to
feel snubbed or slighted by those around him. In fiction of a more
realistic sort, he might have been portrayed as a troubled adolescent who hides his feelings behind the clown's mask. In the Rover
Boys series he remains a stock figure, the practical joker.

In folk and fairy tales, the youngest child is standardly the
focal character, a misprized but deserving Cinderlad or Cinderella. Sam Rover, instead, stays in his brothers' shadows —
he looks just like Tom, Winfield writes in the first book of the
series, and he acts like Dick's stand-in. The only place he stands
out is on the playing fields of Putnam Hall and Brill College,

for he is an extraordinary athlete. (There is perhaps one exception to this statement: in the last book of the first series, *The Rover Boys on a Tour*, Sam assumes a more central role, probably because his brothers are married by this time and thus retired to the wings by a marketwise author.) Possibly Stratemeyer realized that a third protagonist contributed but little, for his next major team of brotherly sleuths, the Hardy Boys, are two in number.

The sons of these three Rovers are typecast, too, and they offer further evidence of how balanced in overall design the two Rover Boys series are. Tom, Dick, and Sam have sons exactly like themselves. Tom's boy Jack is the eldest and is the born leader of the next generation of cousins. Tom energetically sires twins, Andy and Randy, so the second series has a double dose of mischievous fun. Sam's Fred is as faceless as his father and, predictably, plays second-in-command to Jack. (He is literally that in *The Rover Boys under Canvas*, where he is lieutenant of the military camp company Jack is captain of.) The first group of Rovers also produce two daughters, Mary and Martha, but they do not much figure in the second series. More important are Ruth Stevenson, Mary Powell, Alice Strobell, and Annie Larkins — who pair up with the young Rovers in a symmetry as perfect as the simultaneous courtships conducted in the first series.

Rounding out the Rovers' camp is a coterie of school chums whose primary function is to supply comic moments in the adventure drama. There are John "Songbird" Powell, Will "Spud" Jackson, William Philander Tubbs, Fred Garrison, and the German lad Hans Mueller. The second batch of Rovers have a similar supporting cast, which includes the requisite fat boy, Fatty Hendry (Tubbs played this role earlier); the oafish German student, Max Spangler; and assorted others, some of whom are — no surprise — sons of the first crew of secondary characters. The Rovers' world, we can safely conclude, is full of corresponding places and people.

In melodrama, good characters are countered by bad, and as has already been discussed, this is the case in the Rover Boys books. The vast machinery of opposition includes a host of minor villains who appear in only one title and really are no more than interchangeable parts, villains with telltale names such as Blackie

Crowden, Peleg Snuggers, Lew Flapp, Gabe Werner, Antonio Ditini, Nappy Martell, and Slugger Brown (the fathers of the last two are also villainous). But the evildoers to be reckoned with are "regulars"; they come back, title after title, to make life interesting for the Rover Boys. The perennial and primary foes are those found in *Down East*: Dudd Flockley, Sid Merrick, Bart Larkspur, Jerry Koswell, Tad Sobber, and especially Dan Baxter and Josiah Crabtree. Crabtree, in particular, demonstrates a lasting power that is truly remarkable, one which crosses generational lines in the Rover family. At the first series' outset, the irascible schoolteacher makes his entrance demanding silence, a request that immediately sets him against the rowdy Rovers. His opening lines are classic. Tom asks if he is under arrest for setting off a firecracker, and Crabtree replies, "You are. . . . We do not allow dime novels, or eatables, or other things that might harm our pupils."[17] Twenty years later he is still around, having survived loss of job, jail sentences, and numerous personal injuries. Finally, in the last volume, *The Rover Boys Winning a Fortune*, Crabtree, by this time old and broken, is allowed to go his way and the merciful Rovers even supply a small amount of money to keep him from starving. This is what comes of having been forced to play Captain Hook to the Rover Boys' Peter Pan. A lifetime of serving as the loyal opposition — and, like Hook, the adult adversary in a boys' adventure tale — has taken its toll.

The opposition in this series is, by definition, wicked. Curiously enough, however, they are not necessarily incorrigible. In *Down East*, one sees the Rovers' habit of confronting trespassers boldly: sometimes this method results in a confession, optionally accompanied by a sniveling expression of repentance. Dan Baxter presents an interesting example. In *The Rover Boys on the Plains*, Tom expresses his doubts on the subject: "Reform him, Dick! That would be mighty uphill work."[18] But by the very next book in the series, Dan begins to come around, showing good, manly form toward the conclusion of the novel: "I'll take my medicine, no matter how bitter it is." Dick replies gently, "I am sure none of us want to see you suffer — if you want to reform" (*Southern Waters*, p. 219).

Baxter does indeed reform. Later volumes portray him as

a jewelry salesman who presents gifts to and performs minor chores for the Rovers. He was much more manly as a pariah! This change of heart must not be mistaken for something akin to "character growth." Melodramatic mysteries have no place for such intricacy. Rather, the sudden reversal affords direct evidence of the Rovers' omnipotence: they can work wonders on even the blackest of foes.

One last point about characterization in the Rover Boys series is easily overlooked because of the sameness of the stories: the Rovers grow up in the course of the series, though their specific ages are never supplied in any given novel. Hence their passage from boyhood to adolescence to manhood is in itself a plot line that spans all twenty books in the first series and ten in the second, where they still figure, as adults now, in their sons' adventures. Taken as a whole, the series is, then, a *bildungsroman* that depicts the coming of age of three boys.

The *bildungsroman* is a kind of narrative that naturally leads to presentation of the author's ideas on human nature and the proper occupation of mankind. Stratemeyer's Rover Boys books, however, are not overtly didactic. After all, he knew that a key to the success of the twentieth-century series book was that, unlike Abbott's, Alger's, and other boys' fiction of the preceding century, it did *not* preach good manners and right behavior. On occasion the author lapses into the old mode, in his introductions most obviously. The introductory letter in *Down East* contains this plain statement: "I earnestly hope [my novels] will please all my readers and *do them some good* [italics mine]." And in early volumes of the series Winfield here and there belabors his message. After a fight in *The Rover Boys at School*, he remarks: "Now, lest my readers obtain a false impression of my views on this subject, let me state plainly that I do not believe in fights, between boys or otherwise. They are brutal, far from manly, and add nothing to the strength of one's character" (p. 109). But this is not customary.

While Stratemeyer in recognition of his readers' tastes kept direct moralizing out of his storytelling as a rule, the embedded themes in the Rover Boys fiction are hard to miss, unless, of course, you were a boy of the new century caught up in the drama of pursuit and punishment and in the nouveau look of the action (new cars, new bi-planes, new freedom). Readers less swept away by the action will notice that the maturation of the heroes closely parallels Stratemeyer's own course and his moral code, which was instilled by Alger and the other authors he read as a boy. Put simply, industry, forthrightness, and initiative will bring success to the Rovers and, by implication, all wideawake readers of the books.[19]

As has been seen, the Rovers' lives are orderly and balanced — things happen in parallel ways. Boys grow up and marry their youthful sweethearts, live in hooked-together houses, have children just like themselves, all according to some natural time-clock, it would seem. Stratemeyer's vision of life comfortably in check rather than flux extends beyond this presentation of his protagonists' easy road to successful manhood. The world in which they live itself runs according to clear and consistent rules. There are those who attack the established order, but they are doomed to failure and are never admitted to the inner sanctum of the Rover realm. In fact, the highly codified society in the Rover Boys books anticipates the soap-opera scene. The fundamental values and laws that operate in the Rovers' world, like those in soap operas, hold fast, no matter how much psychological distress is inflicted by the bad characters upon the good. The specific setting may change (from school and Cedarville to New York and the wide world), the good characters may be tried and tempted by bad eggs, but the social and moral order is never in question. Thus, ultimately, the manly middle-class representatives of the status quo will triumph.

Stratemeyer was not alone among his contemporaries in this romantic vision of life. Half the top sellers in the fiction market at the turn of the century were "novels of high romance," according to Frank Luther Mott.[20] The western romance was a favorite with the reading public in the first decade of the twentieth century — novels like Owen Wister's *The Virginian* (1902) and Zane Grey's *The Spirit of the Border* (1906). Two of Grey's novels, *The U. P. Trail* and *The Man of the Forest*, would top best-seller lists in later years as well, 1918 and 1920 respectively. The Rovers from time to time took trips and solved mysteries out west, but in their optimistic romantic vision of life all of the Rover volumes were closely related to the westerns read by adults of the day. As William Ruehlmann has commented, in America "the private eye novel was a western that took place somewhere else."[21]

There are two reasons why it was a likely choice for Stratemeyer (or any other author) to write romantic adventure mysteries about adolescents for adolescents. First, the notion of adolescence was a popular and novel subject at the outset of the 1900s. The topic was defined and explored by educator and psychologist G. Stanley Hall in 1904 in his influential two-volume work, *Adolescence: Its Psychology and Its Relations to Physiology, Anthropology, Sociology, Sex, Crime, Religion, and Education.*[22] More important is the fact that romantic literature is ideally suited to depiction of the young. As Northrop Frye notes, romance "is perenially child-like . . . [and] marked by its extraordinarily persistent nostalgia, its search for some kind of imaginative golden age in time or space."[23] The Rover Boys series is Stratemeyer's grown-up and romantic myth of his own youth and of a more youthful America.

In this sense the books are counterparts of such classic romantic adventure tales for boys as *Treasure Island* and *Peter Pan*, or Arthur Ransome's later *Swallows and Amazons.*[24] Some books in the series, like these works, actually take place on an island retreat — for example *The Rover Boys on Land and Sea*, which according to Winfield's introduction centers on escapades "on the sea and on a number of far away islands, where, for a time, all lead a sort of Robinson Crusoe life." But even those that take place closer to school and home depict a romanticized world, where the Rover adolescents are as firmly in charge as Peter Pan is in Neverland. They are on their own, bringing in adult arms of the law only incidentally to assist them, not vice versa. And parents are either nonexistent — the Rovers' mother is dead — or the sort of accommodating guardian the young dream of but seldom have. Anderson Rover not only gives the boys his blessing to roam, he assists them, as in *The Rover Boys on Treasure Isle*. In that tale he luckily has a friend who owns a steam yacht and gladly charters it for the boys and himself to use in cruising the West Indies. Mr. Rover calls the expedition "a fine outing for a summer even if we don't locate Treasure Isle."[25]

It *is* a fine outing, as are the other expeditions depicted elsewhere in the series. And so one comes back around to the Rovers' appeal to young readers. For them, what stood out was the breezy atmosphere of the books — more often than not it is summertime and the living is indeed free and easy — and the racy, no-brakes quality of the Rovers' adventures and mysteries. In the series, textbooks are happily abandoned, family typically left behind, and teachers absent (or perpetually disposed of, in Crabtree's case), all in favor of the unimpeded chase and discovery of secrets. Dennis Porter's comparison of the roller coaster and detective novels perfectly describes the motives for wanting to ride the road with the Rovers:

> both . . . are machines for producing thrills. . . . A reader, like a rider, submits himself willingly to the prepared experiences of a closed-circuit system that promises to return him to the safety of his point of origin after having exposed him to a series of breathtaking dips and curves.[26]

Just as Crabtree disallowed the older dime novels, so books like those in which the Rover Boys appeared were frowned upon by teachers, parents, and the children's book reviewer for *St. Nicholas*. To return to the words of this last authority, "The best romance becomes dangerous if by its excitement it renders the ordinary course of life uninteresting, and increases the morbid thirst for useless acquaintance with scenes in which we shall never be called upon to act." Nonetheless, boys did remain thirsty for the vicarious thrills found in the stories about Rovers and their charmed lives. Lads will develop a propensity for fun, as Winfield would have said. And short of the real thing, what more pleasant recreation could there be than an afternoon spent on a trip with the Rovers?

"Who are you?" she demanded
—*Ruth Fielding and Her Double*
Alice B. Emerson
Cupples and Leon, 1932

4

RUTH FIELDING
Orphan Turned
Hollywood Sleuth

There was the cartridge belt about her waist and the revolver. But to reach the weapon she must alter her position, though ever so slightly. There was the possibility that her numbed fingers might fumble the weapon, might even drop it in the snow. In that case, there would be an end to Ruth Fielding and all her hopes and aspirations.

— *Ruth Fielding in the Far North*

After 1900, series fiction for American girls blossomed. The checklist *Girls Series Books* lists forty-six series begun in the first decade of the century; and ninety-four, between 1910 and 1920, the most productive period to date in terms of popular fiction for girls and female adolescents.[1] School stories and travel adventures and eventually mysteries dominated the new girls' books during these two decades and in the 1920s as well. Some throwbacks to the earlier domestic fiction written for girls and women can be found — *Mrs. Wiggs of the Cabbage Patch, Anne of Green Gables, Pollyanna*, and all the best sellers of Gene Stratton-Porter.[2] But the emerging series fiction presented heroines out in the world. In fact, the number of resourceful orphans seen soloing their way through life in this new fiction documents the shifting cultural perspectives in the Progressive Era. Unlike their predecessors, these young women do not long remain cooped up by the benevolent relatives who take them in. Edward Stratemeyer's Ruth Fielding was the preeminent "charity child" on the go. She starred in thirty titles published by the Syndicate between 1913 and 1934, thereby taking the productivity prize among the some eighteen girls series Stratemeyer invented before his death in 1930.

The first Syndicate series for girls, Dorothy Dale, appeared in 1908. The title of its first volume is noteworthy: *Dorothy Dale, a Girl of Today*.[3] This series was primarily the work of Lillian Garis, as was the second Stratemeyer creation for girls, the Motor Girls, begun in 1910 under the same pen name of Margaret Penrose. Both series depict protagonists who travel to seacoasts and mountains, confront hermits and gypsies, and untangle minor mysteries — in short, they do the things that would become staple activities for adventure series heroines. The Motor Girls, however, is the better indicator of what was new about the twentieth-century girls' series. In it, Cora Kimball and her "wide-awake" chums roam about in a touring car, just like the Rover Boys and Clarence Young's Motor Boys (from whom the Motor Girls were cloned), encountering cases of missing heirlooms and stolen stocks by the bushel basket. This sort of travel adventure story for girls remained immensely popular through the early 1920s. To cite just one somewhat eccentric statistic, five different publishers sold series about Campfire Girls between 1913 and 1921.[4]

The period between 1912 and 1914 ushered in what has been called the Golden Age for Stratemeyer and his Syndicate.[5] Twenty-two Syndicate series were in progress in the three-year span, among them such ongoing hits as the Rover Boys and Tom Swift (begun in 1899 and 1910, respectively) and new offerings like Baseball Joe and the Motion Picture Boys. New girls series made a strong showing at this time, too. The Outdoor Girls, by the Bobbsey Twins' Laura Lee Hope, began in 1913 and continued for twenty years and twenty-three volumes. It was followed by Amy Bell Marlowe's Books for Girls, the Girls of Central High, the Moving Picture Girls, the Corner House Girls, and Ruth Fielding. Some of these series, like the preceding Motor Girls, were direct descendants, or spinoffs, of specific boys' series begun a few years earlier. Even Ruth Fielding, who in so many ways stands alone, was projected by Stratemeyer as a complement to another new entry of 1913, the Speedwell Boys.[6] But as the previous chapters have shown, imitation of past winners was the operative rule at the Stratemeyer Syndicate, and the new girls' books should not be thought of as pale copies of their counterparts for males. In certain respects — the evolution of the mystery pattern foremost among them — the early twentieth-century girls series raced ahead of boys' books.

The Ruth Fielding series was published under the pseudonym Alice B. Emerson, whose fame as Ruth's creator was later drawn upon in advertisements for a follow-up series about another orphan, the Betty Gordon books begun by Emerson in 1920. In reality, the books were, as usual, conceived by Stratemeyer himself, and it is known that some of them were written by W. Bert Foster.[7] Beyond that slim fact, very little has been recorded about either the writing of the Ruth Fielding series or its reception by readers and critics. And while I have found women who well remember reading Ruth's exploits in their youth, the books themselves are much more difficult to come by today (outside research libraries) than are the Rover Boys volumes and even far more obscure early series books. The silence regarding Ruth and her books' disappearance are surprising since the heroine during her heyday certainly lived up to the tall claims made by her publishers, Cupples and Leon: "Ruth Fielding is a character that will live in juvenile fiction." *Within* the world of her series, what is more, the young woman became an internationally celebrated "film scenario" writer, actress, director, and film-company owner. To these roles she added, in good time, those of wife and mother — and famous detective. After an important Hollywood lawyer Ruth has consulted suggests she hire a professional detective to track down an impostor, he immediately retracts his advice: "All right . . . that was merely a suggestion. From what I have heard, the young lady already has a reputation as a detective."[8]

Ruth Fielding deserves to be rediscovered. She is one of the best representatives of her many contemporary series heroines — best because of her series' popularity and because of her own position as a pivotal figure in fiction for American girls. Ruth is the orphan, a carry-over from the nineteenth-century sentimental tradition, turned movie star and sleuth, two new roles for fictional heroines of the 1900s. Further, Ruth's development over the course of thirty books in a society that presents seemingly infinite possibilities is as fascinating as it is confusing in its account of the tensions that arise when a smart girl with old-fashioned values wants to enjoy the new possibilities open to her. Ruth Fielding, in fact, faces compelling dilemmas beyond the predictable problems posed by scheming competitors, petty thieves, and would-be interlopers. The choices she is allowed to, and must, make regarding her personal life and her career are not easy ones, no matter how decisive a character she is cooked up to be or how simply these dilemmas are sometimes written off.

For the very facts outlined above, it is hard to select a representative title in the Ruth Fielding series. Like other girls' series of the period, and boys' books, too, for that matter, this one floundered around seeking a comfortable literary genre to call home. The first volumes are, for the main, school stories; an intermediate group concern vacation travels. These are followed by three books about Ruth Fielding's adventures during the war as a Red Cross nurse. The other half of the series — the last fifteen titles — are stories of Ruth's skyrocketing career in the movie industry and of her personal growth from schoolgirl to single career girl to wife and mother. What is more, at least three-fourths of the series belong to the mystery genre, the narrative formula so many pre-1930 girls' series gradually settled in to. With these qualifications set forth, the summary of an exemplary Ruth Fielding book, *Ruth Fielding at Cameron Hall*, follows.

"There she is! That girl in the blue sweater is Ruth Fielding!"

"You mean the one giving orders through the megaphone? She looks too young to be a moving picture director."[9]

Three younger girls, students at Ruth's alma mater Ardmore College, are in Hollywood, gawking on the set where Ruth Fielding supervises the filming of a picture for which she wrote a prize-winning scenario. The prize amounted to fifty thousand dollars. This, along with the fact that it is Ruth's own company that is doing the filming, is the information provided on page 1 of the volume. The principal character's celebrity status is thus firmly established for all readers, including those few who had not come across one of the twenty-three preceding titles in the series.

After further complimentary remarks about Ruth, the starry-

eyed undergraduates recede, and the production work rolls
into action. In a "curt and businesslike" voice Ruth advises ac-
tors filming a hurricane scene on their facial expression. Helen
Cameron, Ruth's friend and faithful sidekick throughout the
series, steps in and says she admires the way Ruth gives orders,
especially to men. But her tone changes, and she remarks un-
pleasantly, "I guess you're in love with your work more deeply
than with my brother!" (p. 6) On cue Helen's twin and Ruth's
fiancé, Tom Cameron, enters, and after his attempts to put his
arm around Ruth are rebuffed, he continues this line of questioning, "Can't I even look at you? You work all the time now,
so I can't expect to talk to you" (p. 8).

Thus chapter 1 of *Ruth Fielding at Cameron Hall* focuses on
romantic conflict. At the end of the chapter, however, the main
mystery plot is introduced: Mr. Grimes, director of Ruth's film,
presents Tom with a telegram containing word of the grave ill-
ness of the twins' father. They must go home at once.

Home for the Camerons and Ruth Fielding is Cheslow,
which Alice B. Emerson describes only as being located in "one
of the New England states." As Helen and Tom prepare for their
train journey east and Ruth tearfully recalls her long-time discouragement of Tom — "I'm afraid he's almost made up his mind
that my work will always come first — that I'll never marry him"
(p. 12) — the narrator recapitulates the history of the series, beginning at the very beginning when the orphaned Ruth arrived at
the Red Mill to live with her great-uncle, Jabez Potter, and
continuing through Ruth, Helen, and Tom's days at boarding
school, the part Ruth played in the war, Ruth's fledgling career
as a script writer, finally moving onto her organization of the
Fielding Film Company, of which Tom is now treasurer. Emphasis is placed on Ruth's growing dissatisfaction with the also
growing demands of her work. When readers are returned to the
present tense of the novel, they find Ruth making short work of
the stack of fan mail and "attractive business propositions" on
her desk: she intends to head for Cheslow herself and help her
friends.

Bad news abounds there. Not only is Mr. Cameron's health
flickering fast, but it turns out the Farmers Savings Bank of
Cheslow has gone under because of bad farm loans followed by

a robbery. This event has special significance for Ruth, who had forty thousand dollars of her prize money in the bank. She vows to see that the robbers don't get away with her cash. It is then implied that she is able and ready to follow up whatever "clews" materialize, for she is the owner and skillful driver of her own roadster, bought because Helen and Tom convinced her that since she was now "somebody" she should not waste time with public transportation! Another mystery is tacked onto the plot at this point in the narrative: Tom and his blue roadster disappear.

As a sleuth, Ruth is as sure of herself as she has always been in other endeavors. Realizing that Tom is fast becoming a suspect in the robbery case, she takes it upon herself to suppress important evidence — namely, a sweater and a cap matching the description of what one of the robbers wore, articles she finds in the Camerons' garage. She is certain of Tom's innocence, and that is reason enough for her action. Besides, she has no confidence in the ability of Sheriff Si Perkins to solve the crime. He aggravates her to the point that she must resist the urge to "reach out and shake the man" (p. 54).

Chapter 8 presents yet another catastrophe. The Lumano River floods its banks, and Ruth must wade through ankle-deep water at the Red Mill to save her uncle's chickens. This natural disaster serves as proof of the young woman's perseverance: "Ruth was determined that she would not allow discouragement to overcome her. Things would come out all right. . . . She would make them come out that way!" (p. 69)

The mystery plot here begins to boil, new clues and baffling events balancing one another suspensefully. Two professional detectives arrive in town and are quick to regard Tom as the most likely suspect. Ruth and Chess Copley, Helen's beau who completes the quartet of series mainstays, begin a search of local farms and discover Tom's car at the bottom of a ravine. Ruth turns deathly pale but is not incapacitated for long. In fact, she announces almost at once, "I have a theory," and begins examining the ground for tracks. Of course, she finds some — ones made by airplane wheels.

This revelation *does* sap her vitality, as do her crochety uncle's insinuations about Tom's guilt. Ruth loses weight and sheds tears over her treatment of Tom. But the mystery investigation seems to propel itself. A trusted stunt man Ruth knows from Hollywood, Jack Markham, comes on the scene. From his plane, he spies a broken airplane rudder in a field and three armed men. This time Ruth calls in the law. The chase is on, Ruth giving all the directions about who will ride in which car.

Ruth and Markham lead a procession of six cars of armed men — Ruth, too, asks the sheriff for a revolver — over rough roads at dusk to the site Markham has seen from his plane. The girl is doing the driving: "She bent low over the wheel, and settled down for the arduous and dangerous ride" (p. 158). Markham is impressed with her nerve and remarks to himself: "Sheer grit! . . . Not many girls could drive the way she can!" In the end the desperadoes are taken, but there is no sign of Tom. Then Ruth finds a trapdoor in the hideout cabin, which leads her to her bound and gagged boyfriend. She kisses him impulsively, and even Tom is convinced her attitude toward him has finally changed.

A conventional exposition of the mystery is provided not by detective Ruth, but by the victimized Tom. This point bears mentioning, for it is a reminder that *Ruth Fielding at Cameron Hall* is not a story of detection accomplished by logical deduction, all Ruth's talk of theories and "thinking things out" notwithstanding.

But the novel is not yet over. Two chapters remain, and in these the romantic narrative assumes the foreground it occupied at the outset of the book. Ruth confesses she hasn't given her work a serious thought since Tom's disappearance and that she thinks she'll take a long rest. To confirmed readers of the series the latter statement will sound familiar, but this time Ruth is not merely hypothesizing. She agrees to marry Tom, and, indeed, the marriage takes place in chapter 25. The wedding is attended by Helen and Chess, an assortment of old school chums, and Mr. Hammond (a film company president who has been Ruth's guardian angel throughout her professional development). Asked when she will return to the movies, Ruth meekly responds, "Not until Tom says I may" (p. 205). Tom enters the picture to assure that he is not a tyrannical husband: he has agreed that in the film world his wife will keep her own name "as dozens of others are doing." Then the two drive off in a new roadster, Tom doing the driving this time:

"The fade out," Helen whispered.

The silence was broken by Ann Hicks, who softly added the title lines:

"'And they rode away, hand in hand, into the sunset.'"

THE END

Ruth Fielding at Cameron Hall represents the climax of the romantic overplot that spans individual volumes of the series, thereby providing a narrative thread for the ongoing depiction of a character who, book by book, grows from a child into a woman. At the same time this volume illustrates what became of girls' adventure series by the early 1920s: they had metamorphosed into mystery novels. By the time the Fielding series adopted the structure and the accoutrement of detective fiction, a fait accompli as early as 1915, mysteries by and primarily for women were gaining popularity with American readers. Much of this literature belonged to the sensational Gothic tradition of heroines sequestered in scary houses and circumstances; but there was also a more public, more social strain, and it concerned characters — sometimes young women no older than Ruth Fielding in *Cameron Hall* — who mingled in the wide world beyond the home and became enmeshed in puzzling cases in the process. In 1914, Hugh C. Weir published *Miss Madelyn Mack, Detective*. As his title intimates, Weir's detective is a professional. A college girl confronted with earning her own living, she systematically sets about gaining a reputation in freelance detection and later opens her own agency — and buys a chalet on the Hudson with the proceeds from her business. One year later Anna Katherine Green's collection of short mysteries, *The Golden Slipper*, introduced Violet Strange, a socialite who takes up employment with a detective agency to finance her sister's singing career. By 1917 the queen of Gothic mysteries, Mary Roberts Rinehart, was spoofing the up-and-coming tradition of the modern Girl Detective, with her "small but powerful car," in *Bab: A Sub-Deb*.[10]

These fictional detectives are comic figures or, at least, flamboyantly eccentric ones (Madelyn Mack, for example, always dresses either in all white or all black), and the problems they solve are often nothing but contrived parlor games. In girls' series books, by contrast, the sleuths and the puzzles they encounter are meant to be taken seriously. When the Outdoor Girls find a suspicious box in the sand during an outing at the shore, it soon leads them to international diamond smugglers; and eventually the U.S. Secret Service must take over the investigation.[11] In *The Camp Fire Girls at the Seashore*, the mystery is no idle divertissement: the girls uncover attempts to deny an heiress her rightful and much-needed fortune.[12] Likewise, Ruth Fielding is a girl detective whose sleuthing contains a strong measure of social action. Plots that may initially appear to be simple tales of kidnapping, theft, or forgery often provide Ruth the opportunity to mete out reward and punishment to their deserving recipients in Orphan Annie fashion. Beneath the suspenseful surface-level action, then, resides a slumbering but clear-cut value system in which good manners, clean living, and hard work earn success, while laziness and a disregard for conventional moral principles spell failure. There is even an undercurrent of noblesse oblige; once she has earned prominence, Ruth uses her position to help "civilize" — or give them the chance to pursue the American dream — promising gypsy boys and Indian maidens. It was not, of course, Stratemeyer's outright intention to convey his conservative themes in stories that for all appearances are merely entertaining "reads." Nonetheless, such thematic infiltration was a side effect the books had on readers caught up in the excitement of the mystery plots.

From their inception, the Ruth Fielding stories cohered: instead of the chain of rapid and random adventures found in the first Rover Boys novels, these narratives had a certain progression or sense of direction. In *Ruth Fielding on Cliff Island*, published in 1915, Ruth's winter vacation trip to a classmate's lodge on Cliff Island quickly turns into an exercise in recovering hidden treasure for its genuine inheritor, a search in which Ruth excels at questioning witnesses and thinking through mysterious happenings. Even the second title in the series, *Ruth Fielding at Briarwood Hall*, contains a definite mystery subplot. To the formulaic boarding school story, full of club initiations, after-hours dorm parties, taffy pulls, and the like, is added an absorbing tale of a marble harp that twangs eerily at night, foreign musicians, and a blackmailed teacher.[13] Later, after Ruth has grown up, the mysteries center

on the film community: rival companies secretly seek to disparage
Ruth's work, or they plot to scoop her exotic locations and pla-
giarize her winning scenarios. Sometimes she simply runs into
a mystery while on a pleasure trip taken with the hopes of getting away from it all. For example, the thirtieth and last book
of the series, *Ruth Fielding and Her Crowning Victory*, concerns
Ruth's involvement in the political intrigue brewing in the king-
dom of Bellogia, a plot she walks into while taking a round-the-
world vacation.

The writing in the Ruth Fielding series does little to impede
the development and eventual unraveling of the mystery plots.
Bobbie Ann Mason has said of the Stratemeyer Syndicate output that the books read inoffensively precisely because of their
sparse style: "The series are so carefully styleless that you can't
point to bad puns, strained metaphors, overloaded descriptions.
There is an absence of language: there is vocabulary, but not
language."[14] This "invisible" style is something that evolved over
the years, and even then Syndicate writers occasionally made
themselves heard through the formulaic styleless patina. But in
the Fielding books, especially when compared with previous
Stratemeyer series like the Rover Boys, there are the beginnings
of that stylelessness Mason refers to. Consequently, the narrative
tone in these books, due largely to the combination of colorless,
seemingly machine-made writing with daring and suspenseful
action, is one of unflappability. The wildest ride, the most fright-
ening moment, the most pregnant romantic conversation — all
sail by in the telling with little embellishment on the part of Alice
B. Emerson. Such coolness has the effect of heightening the thrills
of the chase, just as understatement can drive a point home.

The tone just described results in large part from the attitude
and actions of the character at the center of the series. While she
is no flapper, Ruth Fielding is a thoroughly contemporary heroine. Among the au courant pasttimes Ruth engages in (beyond
the films and automobiling) are airplane piloting and swimming.
Five years after Amelia Earhart set out over the Atlantic, Ruth
rescues Pacific islanders caught in a fire.[15] Gertrude Ederle swam
the English Channel in 1926; Ruth's accomplishments in this area
are more modest — she saves drowning people thanks to her study

of American Red Cross lifesaving. And her personal style mirrors the casual, flippant attitude of her day. Even in her youth she was known to remark "dryly" upon occasion, and she never gushed in the manner of young heroines in domestic novels. Her playful conversation as an adult woman with husband Tom has the ring of the bantering repartee between Nick and Nora Charles in Dashiell Hammett's *The Thin Man*, published in 1934, the last year a new Ruth Fielding title was issued. In sum, Ruth is no-nonsense, unsentimental, independent, aggressive, ambitious, and assertive. On the other hand, she sometimes frets about how others think of her, worries about how she treats Tom, and eventually subscribes to (or attempts to subscribe to) traditional Victorian notions of women and family. Like many young women over fifty years later, then, she can be "conflicted" regarding her right social roles and her relationships with those around her.[16]

In her series Ruth is surrounded by the usual galleries of supporters and detractors. The second category includes a wide assortment of stereotypes common to Stratemeyer's and other series fiction: gypsy thieves, Italian extortionists, Mexican troublemakers, opium-smuggling "Chinamen." In this series there are, in addition, rival filmmakers, along with more nondescript robbers like those seen in *Cameron Hall*. All these inherently evil figures are immediately recognizable when they come into the scene. Here is a standard introduction of villains:

> Evidently they were hands on board the ship. One was a short, stocky fellow with bulging forehead and outthrust jaw and with little eyes set like black beads on either side of a bulbous nose. The other was more commonplace in appearance, being of medium height and sandy complexion, but his eyes were shifty and furtive.[17]

Readers can always identify antagonists by their eyes.

Interestingly, there are villainesses in the Fielding books — Stratemeyer was too chivalrous to write about evil women in his Rover Boys series. The female enemies of Ruth Fielding are typically grasping or would-be actresses, women with names like Maizie Duckworth, Viola Casselle, and Mrs. Craven-Spitz. It should also be noted that nature offers its share of danger and opposition, as the incident recounted in the epigraph to this chapter demonstrates: the foes Ruth is about to shoot are two bears. Elsewhere she battles floods, black panthers, and brush fires. In this respect her exploits parallel those of her contemporary serial film stars — she endures and triumphs over the "perils of Pauline."[18]

In her camp cheering her on are Ruth's lifelong friends, whom she met during her school days. Helen Cameron is always at her chum's side; a newlywed in *Ruth Fielding and Her Double*, she abandons her husband to take a cross-country train trip with Ruth. More minor series regulars appear from time to time in the progression of the thirty books: the jolly fat girl, Jennie "Heavy" Stone, who by *Ruth Fielding on the St. Lawrence* (1922) has married a dashing French soldier; Ann Hicks, a western girl with rough edges; Mary Cox; Nettie Parsons from Louisiana; and the crippled Mercy Curtis, a type left over from children's books of an earlier era. Mercy (nicknamed "Goody Two-Sticks") has mercifully been dropped in later books like *Cameron Hall*.

Among the adult population of the series, Ruth's Uncle Jabez, the miller who took the girl in at the beginning of her saga, and his loyal housekeeper, Alvirah Boggs, are also on her side. But Jabez Potter occasionally behaves in such a miserly and mean-spirited fashion toward her that Ruth is reduced to tears. He can thus be viewed as a member of another class of characters important in the Fielding series, male authority figures. Rich and powerful men are plentiful in Ruth's adventures and mysteries, from Helen and Tom's father, Mr. Macy Cameron, to Mr. Hammond, the chief of Alectrion Film Corporation and Ruth's benefactor in Hollywood. Other male film directors and producers crop up as well. Some help Ruth attain her goals, others chafe at her success. All in all, Ruth holds her own with these characters.

Tom Cameron is, unquestionably, Ruth's most ardent supporter. He, and Chess Copley to a lesser degree, occupies a far more central position in the action of this series than did the girls in the Rover Boys books. Initially, Tom and the other boys on hand during Ruth's school days are simply trimming: they help the girls climb up steep rocks, for example. Romantic interest is nil. When a group composed of both sexes is stuck in a cave for the night in *Ruth Fielding on Cliff Island*, they pass the time by playing games, singing songs, and — unbelievable as it may seem — writing a "burlesque history of 'George Washington and the Cherry Tree.'"[19] Four books later, readers learn that Ruth takes a levelheaded, virtually indifferent attitude toward the opposite sex: "As for Ruth herself, she considered boys no mystery. She was fond of Tom. . . . Other boys did not interest Ruth in the least."[20] But in time Tom becomes more than Ruth's close friend and confidant. He takes on the roles of eager (and repeatedly rebuffed) suitor, treasurer of the Fielding Film Company, Ruth's leg man in games of detection, and ultimately her husband and the father of her child. In other words, Tom changes as much as the heroine in the series' twenty-one-year history, but he remains her satellite, his path and his mood dictated by her latest turn. Still, as *Cameron Hall* makes clear, he eventually breaks through Ruth's sometimes icy façade; indeed, in some of the volumes she is plagued by guilt feelings concerning him.

To return to the series's title character, Ruth Fielding is a forthright and free-spirited exemplar of the era in which she first appeared in 1913. One of the clearest indicators of her independence is her status as sole heroine of a series. Though there were certainly other solitary female protagonists in early series books for girls, the characters for the most part traveled in groups: The Motor Girls, the Outdoor Girls, and the Girls of Central High, among Stratemeyer's series, and the Fairmount Girls, the High School Girls, all the Campfire Girls, the College Girls, and the Khaki Girls, among other offerings. Not until after 1930 was it uncommon to find in series fiction clusters of girls sharing adventures. Furthermore, some of Ruth's contemporaries — the Motor Girls and the Outdoor Girls — live a life of leisure. It is daddy's money, more often than not, that provides them with their touring cars, their chocolates, and the time to amuse themselves with mystery adventures. Ruth, by contrast, follows a long line of fictional females who must depend either on the charity of those beyond immediate family or on their own devices to get by, and the orphan is a solitary by definition.[21]

There is, however, a fundamental difference between Ruth Fielding and the majority of her prototypes. They are Cinderellas who sometimes must submit to others' supervision and not always kind treatment (young Jane Eyre has to tolerate being locked in the Red Room because of her conduct toward John Reed), but Ruth is never a prisoner at Uncle Jabez's Red Mill. From the first book of the series, she sets about shaping her own circumstances. In this regard she resembles another character in nineteenth-century girls' books, the high-spirited and intelligent tomboy like Alcott's Jo March. However, since social expectations were starting to change after 1900, Ruth is not considered boyish because she likes activity and mental challenge and plans to achieve her dreams in the world beyond hearth and home.

When she arrives at the Red Mill after the death of her parents, Ruth *is*, in Jabez Potter's view, the misprized, unfortunate Cinderella. To readers, too, her predicament in *Ruth Fielding of the Red Mill* may seem as bleak as was Dorothy's in *The Wonderful Wizard of Oz*. Both are stuck with old and gray relatives. In neither case were they stuck for long, as it turns out. According to the publisher's publicity for the Fielding book, "her sunny disposition melted the old miller's heart." In fact, it was Ruth's resourcefulness in recovering his cash box that improved her lot, for Uncle Jabez agreed to send her to boarding school as a repayment for her services. In the eighth title in the series, Ruth again betters her condition, this time by earning a five-thousand-dollar reward when she returns a pearl necklace to its owner. That book ends with a statement regarding the girl's future:

> Her life stretched before her over a much pleasanter path than ever before.
> Her own future seemed secure. She could prepare herself for college and could gain the education she craved. It seemed that nothing could balk her ambition.[22]

Later Ruth uses other talents not just to secure her place but to advance it. In *Ruth Fielding in Moving Pictures*, she confesses, "I'm just *mad* to try writing a scenario for a moving picture."[23] So she does, winning a twenty-five dollar prize and the production of her picture. By 1927, in *Ruth Fielding and Her Great Scenario*, the stakes are considerably higher: Ruth wins a fifty-thousand-dollar prize for her script and gets to shoot the picture herself. Orphans sometimes are viewed with sympathy, but in Ruth

Fielding's case there is clearly no cause. Instead, she commands respect, as seen at the beginning of *Cameron Hall*:

> "Miss Fielding owns her own company and finances it herself. . . . Isn't she lucky? Wish I were in her shoes!"
> "Lucky? It's brains and pluck! I consider it a privilege just to say we went to the same college she did, even if she graduated before we entered." (p. 2)

Actually, it was luck and brains and pluck. Like Horatio Alger's heroes, Ruth is industry, initiative, and imagination incarnate—but she also shares with them the uncanny knack of being in the right place at the right time.

When it comes to temperament and emotional tendencies, Ruth again represents the new age. From the outset her physical and emotional health are emphasized: in *Cliff Island* readers are told she is "particularly free from 'nerves'" (p. 181). And her manner is surely a marked departure from that of the fainting heroines in previous sentimental domestic fiction. There is nothing faint-hearted or self-pitying about Ruth Fielding; even her voice is described as "caressing not lachrymose." Yet Alice B. Emerson makes it plain that Ruth is not cold, shallow, or supercilious (her cavalier treatment of Tom notwithstanding), as were some of the new fictional heroines in adult novels of detection. She is known to cry when a friend or colleague mistreats her, and she can become extremely frightened in the face of danger even as she displays remarkable courage and self-possession. Throughout her life, what is more, she befriends the unfortunate with as much energy as she pursues her own goals.

In looks Ruth Fielding alters appreciably as the series progresses. Initially she is the hardy schoolgirl, vivacious but not beautiful, "plump, but not too plump." Frontispieces and covers of the early volumes in the series picture a young woman in a middy blouse, long skirt, and stockings. Down the line, in the 1920s and early 1930s, Ruth is svelte and glamorous in her dropped-waist dresses or tailored suits and cloche hats. This physical change is, of course, natural since she does grow up within the series. It is also an objectification of the extraordinary ascent of the young orphan become "famous authoress of canned drama," reowned sleuth, wife, and mother. Readers follow Ruth as she, by degrees, moves up the ladder of success — and they witness her confidence and her abilities growing apace. Ruth's development is calibrated far more distinctly than was that of the Rovers, who quietly became men "between the scenes," as it were, much as characters died offstage in Renaissance drama. Of course, Ruth is *not* the sort of realistically rounded character E. M. Forster described (Stratemeyer's books did not contain such figures), but she does actually change and progress, giving the series a narrative momentum of its own.

Discussion of Ruth Fielding's maturation and of the significant changes she undergoes in her personal life brings up the issue of what kind of popular fiction the Fielding books are. They are, first and foremost, mystery adventures and the romantic plot line that evolves as Ruth grows up remains a subplot to the mystery in any given book. In *Cameron Hall*, for instance, the romantic plot brackets the more fully developed mystery, moving to the foreground only in the first and last chapters of the book and otherwise serving to supply motivation for Ruth's frantic sleuthing. In the girls' series books that emerged in the 1930s and remained popular through the early 1960s, the romantic elements often seem as important as the mysteries heroines encounter in the course of their work — such career mystery series as the popular Connie Blair, Vicki Barr, and Cherry Ames books.[24] Ruth Fielding, by contrast, thinks of herself as a school/career girl or a detective out to uncover wrongful deeds, a priority Tom Cameron is sometimes painfully aware of even after he persuades Ruth to become his wife. And the primary career and mystery aspects of Fielding novels are usually integrated, for many of the mysteries Ruth solves *must* be cleared up to preserve her professional standing — she exposes an inferior actress who poses as her double; she repeatedly tracks down malevolent competitors who seek to ruin her or steal her material.

Ruth's concern to preserve her reputation points to another significant dimension of her series: its worldly setting. Yes, initially the heroine is an ordinary orphan living near the obscure New England town of Cheslow and going to school at the equally obscure Briarwood Hall and, later, Ardmore College. But as soon as she writes her first screen scenario, she is catapulted into the bright lights of Hollywood and remains ever after a famous personage. There is no escaping her celebrity status no matter where she goes. In fact, when she travels it is usually on business (for example, to an exotic location she intends to use as a backdrop for a film). All the world is her territory, and all its citizens her admirers. As for the nature of this world in which she moves, it reflects the actual world in which Ruth Fielding books were made and sold as surely as the series protagonist represents the wishes and dreams of her readers. It is an exciting place, affording opportunity for immense success — and failure. The stakes are great but so are the risks. That is, Ruth's world is not nearly as safe or predictable as the Rovers' sphere. She moves to the top of the glittering film industry, but she also travels to the war front, nearly loses her money in a bank failure, and has her own baby kidnapped.[25]

Given Ruth's spectacular mobility (both geographical and social) and her access to the risks, mysteries, and opportunities of the wide world, there is ultimately no way the character could be read by girls and young women as one of them. As schoolgirls, Helen and Ruth had admired actresses on location at their college. Tom reminds them, "Pooh! . . . they don't let girls like you play in movies" (*Moving Pictures*, p. 7). In general — that is, in Helen's and most readers' cases — he is probably right, but Ruth is no ordinary American girl. The adventures and mysteries in which she gets involved were normally several cuts more sophisticated than the adventures even the most up-to-date readers encountered (or those happened upon by the Motor Girls, Betty Gordon, or others). Consequently, she must be viewed at some distance by admiring readers. The author assists in creating this distance, moreover, by continual reference to "her" character by full name. "To think was to act with Ruth Fielding" is a pet statement — or, "Intuition was strong in Ruth Fielding." Tom even kisses "Ruth Fielding."

If the Ruth Fielding series were filmed (Nick Carter's stories were), Ruth would be pictured at no closer than medium range; and long-range panoramic shots in which she faces overwhelming adversity gallantly would be plentiful, as they are in the frontispieces of the novels. The camera angle would be from down under, looking up at the superstar. Readers are given a similar perspective in the books. Like consumers of today's celebrity magazines, their voyeuristic impulses are appealed to: they are urged to peek at, even though they must watch from afar, what the glamorous are up to. The nature of the appeal Ruth Fielding had for her readers was tampered with in the last eight volumes of the series. Its demise was due in large part to this tampering.

Ruth Fielding's appeal as a celebrated and extraordinary heroine whom girl readers could look up to suffered from the moment she got married, at the end of *Ruth Fielding at Cameron Hall*. Why weren't marriage and family compatible with her work and her detection? The problem was not one of narrative or plot conflict; the romantic overplot that evolved at the series level remained a generally unobtrusive subplot within individual volumes, where mystery-adventure action predominated. The discord, instead, stemmed from the tension Ruth's two lives, the personal and the professional, created regarding her characterization.

The Stratemeyer Syndicate tried to have it both ways in the seven books that followed *Cameron Hall*. The conflicts regarding her gender roles, long incipient in Ruth's mind, are magnified, growing to almost grotesque proportions at times in these last novels. Hence she becomes a borderline schizophrenic. She repeatedly proclaims her complete submission to Tom and family life, as in *Ruth Fielding in Talking Pictures*:

> "Don't worry, dear," he said, half-banteringly. "Helen wanted to be kidnapped this time. Just as you did on your wedding day. And I warn you that Chess and I are going to do a better job of holding you than those Mexican actors did. We'll keep you and Helen forever Prisoners in the Tower of Love. You'll never escape."
>
> "We'll never want to, Tom!"[26]

Elsewhere, on the other hand, she passionately defends her work. As soon as she and Tom return from their European honeymoon, they have this heated discussion:

> "Hollywood is in your blood, I guess." Tom sighed, as

though reconciled to his fate. "You haven't been the same since we stepped off the train and you sniffed the moving picture atmosphere. You have more money now than you can ever use, and more honor than you want. I don't see why you go on directing pictures. The work's too hard, Ruth. I wish you could take life easy."

"But I work because I love it, Tom. Work doesn't seem hard when you're absorbed in it."[27]

At times these dual perspectives intersect in behavior that seems, well, a bit twisted. In *Ruth Fielding and Baby June* the protagonist applies all her ambition, energy, and resourcefulness toward seeing to it that her daughter June takes first place in a baby parade!

What has happened to Ruth's character does, ultimately, make for irreconcilable structural — actually, genre — differences in the Ruth Fielding series. John Cawelti has written that the feminine equivalent of the adventure story, the narrative most popular with male readers, is the romance.[28] The genre of romance, he continues, favors the "Cinderella formula" in which the poor heroine falls in love with a rich man. We have seen that Ruth Fielding is one orphan who determinedly avoids this scenario: she writes her own script as a canny heroine who thinks through the puzzles she encounters on the road to fame and fortune. In so doing, she challenges Cawelti's contention, for her series belongs squarely to the adventure saga, not the romance classification . . . until the last volumes. Then, like its heroine, it is two-edged.

The working out, or resolution, of the personal side of Ruth's story *does* conform with a variant of the formulaic romance. Ruth's marriage follows Cawelti's description of a more contemporary romance formula in which a career girl "rejects love in favor of wealth or fame, only to discover that love alone is fully satisfying." The problem in Ruth's case is that she does and she doesn't believe that last premise. Like Dorothy, who came back to Kansas transformed by her experiences and trials in the magical world of Oz, Ruth Fielding settles down to a quiet family life imbued with the strength of her conquests and discoveries in the wide world, and the desire for more such excitement. And the result is unsettling, for both her and her readers, who had come to expect in a Fielding title the tale of an independent and glamorous supergirl.

How did the creators of this series get themselves in such a bind by the end of the 1920s? Their own social context was a chief cause. This was a confusing time when it came to questions of women's place. Demands for female equality had culminated in the gaining of women's suffrage in 1920; yet despite media talk of the New Woman the twenties were quiescent years for women, many of whom turned to seeking personal fulfillment in their lives through traditional family structures, liberated quests for gratification, or some combination of both. As historian T. J. Jackson Lears has remarked, "the emphasis [in the 1920s] on self-realization through emotional fulfillment [and] the devaluation of public life in favor of a leisure world of intense private experience . . . helped to domesticate the drive toward female emancipation."[29] Ruth Fielding reflects the changing, uncertain attitudes of the period.

She is not alone in her confusion. Contemporary heroines in the more critically respectable girls' books of the 1920s and 1930s, many of whom literally live on the frontier, express similar ambivalence about the female role. Carol Ryrie Brink's Caddie Woodlawn, Kate Seredy's Cousin Kate, and Constance Skinner's Becky Landers — all these girls are dubious about the idea of growing up if it means assuming the role of the traditional "lady."[30] In her youth Ruth had no such qualms, for she knew she would grow up to do exactly what she chose. But her later conflict as an adult woman demonstrated that even when enormous talent, strong character, and indomitable will are available, there was reason for girls to be unsure. "Having it all" — interesting work, marriage, and children — didn't come easily.

Edward Stratemeyer, of course, did not intend to involve his heroine in this quandary. His value system was simple enough: no doubt he wanted to portray a happy blend of the old-fashioned, family-oriented female in whom he believed and the new young woman on the go who would thrill readers. Unfortunately the combination did not gel, and even Stratemeyer seemed aware of the incongruity. In *Cameron Hall* and its successors considerable attention is paid to smoothing over the problem — e.g., repeated discussion of Ruth's retaining her own name for professional purposes. Once, Alice B. Emerson has Ruth state emphatically:

"Getting married shouldn't make a person feel serious. Just look at us. We're positively giddy at times" (*Clearing Her Name*, p. 23). True enough, but the nature of the adventure series was altered so dramatically that it lost direction, judging from the way in which the last Ruth Fielding books make half-hearted stabs at starting off anew. Some self-consciously underline in language and props their connection with the up-and-coming detective novel; and the last title, *Ruth Fielding and Her Crowning Victory*, is a strange excursion into fantasy, concerning as it does the royal circles of two imaginary European kingdoms. But as the title of that book intimates, the series had run its course. Ruth is, at last, right when she tells Tom at the end of the novel:

> "This time I'm home never more to roam," she said softly.
> "I've heard that before," Tom chuckled.
> "But now I really mean it. If there are any more adventures in our little family, they will be passed on to June!"[31]

The orphan was home to stay, and the series was over.

Ruth Fielding could not be brought out of the dilemma I have described. But Stratemeyer Syndicate personnel did learn some lessons from Ruth's predicament that they could apply to future series. First, they should freeze their protagonists in time by not allowing them to age. This practice had worked before in a number of nonseries juvenile novels. *Rebecca of Sunnybrook Farm*, for example, ends: "And she [Rebecca]? Her own future was close-folded still; folded and hidden in beautiful mists."[32] Second, the Syndicate learned to restrict their characters spatially — namely, to distance them from the options and dilemmas of the real world. When Ruth left the havens of the Red Mill and Ardmore College and became successful and famous in the world beyond, she could never come home again — and be happy with the garden-variety adventures that setting would offer. Both these lessons were kept in mind during the conception of two new series that were beginning just as Ruth Fielding flagged. The Hardy Boys and Nancy Drew have remained teenagers for nearly sixty years now, and they still live in those secluded never-never lands of Bayport and River Heights.

"That's the smugglers' code!" Frank exclaimed. "Not motor numbers at all!"

—*The Phantom Freighter*
Franklin W. Dixon
Grosset and Dunlap, 1947

5

THE HARDY BOYS
Soft-Boiled Detection

"I'll guarantee that if I visit here much longer I'll see that those two boys haven't much chance for more detectiving!" she announced. "I'll cure 'em, so I will. It's no business at all for boys."

. . .

"You're welcome to try, Aunt Gertrude," said Mr. Hardy; "but I'm afraid you'll never cure my sons of wanting to be detectives. I've set them the example, you see."

"More's the pity," sniffed Aunt Gertrude. "Why couldn't you have been a plumber? It's safer."

"But not as exciting," said Fenton Hardy, with a laugh.

— The Missing Chums

In 1984 Franklin W. Dixon's eightieth volume in the Hardy Boys series, *The Roaring River Mystery*, was published. Frank and Joe Hardy are about to begin their seventh decade of crime solving today, over seventy million Hardy Boys novels have been purchased, and in the last three years over two and a half million paperback copies of their mysteries were sold—not bad for a series one critic called "nothing more than updated Rover."[1] It is true that the first Hardy Boys title, *The Tower Treasure*, appeared in 1927, one year after the last Rover Boys book. Of more significance, I would say, is the fact that the Hardy Boys were conceived exactly as detective novels by American writers burst onto the market. S. S. Van Dine published *The Benson Murder Case* in

1926; John Dickson Carr, *It Walks by Night* in 1929; and two cousins, Frederic Dannay and Manfred B. Lee, writing under the pseudonym Ellery Queen, *The Roman Hat Mystery*, also in 1929.[2] Even more important was the emergence in the mid-twenties of the tough-sounding American strain of the mystery genre in pulp magazines such as *Black Mask*. There, writers like Carroll John Daly, Charles M. Green (a.k.a. Erle Stanley Gardner), Dashiell Hammett, and Raymond Chandler wrote what has come to be known generally as the "hard-boiled" brand of detective fiction. The Hardy Boys are clearly connected to this boom in the popularity of detection among the adult reading public in America.

The Hardys, of course, do owe something to the boys' books that preceded them at the Edward Stratemeyer Syndicate. The character Frank Hardy actually dates back to 1905; his name, at least, is found in one of the Horatio Alger novels worked on by Stratemeyer.[3] Frank and Joe Hardy have more pronounced affinities with the Rovers, the Motor Boys, the Speedwell Boys, and Victor Appleton's contemporary Don Sturdy, all of whom are actively engaged in the travel adventure. In 1910, Edward Stratemeyer said, "Automobiling is to-day one of the best of our sports. This writer is himself the fortunate possessor of a touring-car, and during the time this story was being written enjoyed numerous trips around his home and beyond."[4] Apparently, the same philosophy held in 1926 when he began writing the Hardy Boys books, only the means of transportation had been multiplied. Quintessentially mobile, the Hardys are car lovers — the convertible was their chosen style for years — but in the course of their sleuthing they also travel by motorcycle, motor boat, iceboat, airplane, and, in the title I'll focus on below, Chinese junk. It is worth noting that the other novels the Syndicate published under the Franklin W. Dixon name were the Ted Scott Flying series.

There is, furthermore, a resemblance between the two Hardys and James Cody Ferris's X Bar X Boys, whose series was started in 1926. Roy and Teddy Manley were billed by Grosset and Dunlap, publishers of the series, as "real cowboys, on the job when required but full of fun and daring." Though fashioned as western heroes, these two brothers form a team of crack explorers, who uncover the schemes of kidnappers, rustlers, and other shady western entrepreneurs. A solitary male detective, Nat Ridley, had also been introduced in a paperback series in 1926.[5] Still, the Hardy Boys hold the distinction of being Stratemeyer's first all-star juvenile characters born as detectives. (Earlier adventurers like the Rovers gradually drifted into mysterious plots.) Aunt Gertrude's threat, quoted above, is in vain. Fenton Hardy is right: "detectiving" is in their blood.

The historical development of the Hardy Boys series looks like the genealogy of a very fertile clan. TV shows, coloring books, comic books, and cartoons have been spawned by the novels. The individual titles themselves have been reprinted; and all those written before 1959, substantially revised. This extended family will be discussed in chapter 7. As for authorship, Edward Stratemeyer planned and wrote the series until his death in 1930, but a number of others have necessarily contributed to this long-running success story — among them, Leslie McFarlane, Harriet Stratemeyer Adams, and Arthur Svenson. The series is now carried on by a determinedly inconspicuous Syndicate staff.

The covers of the first series volumes are khaki in color and carry, emblazoned in brown, the silhouette of two boys on the prowl on a stormy night. One wears a hat and tie, both have on baggy trousers. Illustrations for the early books likewise depict wavy-haired youth in wide-collared shirts, sweater vests, or full-cut suits. By the late 1950s, Frank and Joe had taken on a new look, younger, clean-cut, more casual; and V-neck sweaters and short hair had replaced pre-World War II fashions. In the 1970s, the boys' hair became tousled. Covers of the current volumes picture preppies in oxford cloth or knit shirts, corduroy pants, even boating shoes. These superficial changes are paralleled by stylistic streamlining of the texts of the Hardy Boys books.

In recent titles there is far less use of dialect and slang in characters' speech, and the occasional stilted phrasing found initially has been ironed out. No such narration as this inelegant passage from the 1932 *While the Clock Ticked* would be printed today: "The boys warmly agreed that jail was much too good for the driver who had so nearly run them down; but as there was nothing they could do about it, the car having vanished before they could take down the number, they dusted their garments and went on their way again."[6] The author's voice, moreover, is sub rosa compared with the chatty persona that used to be. *Footprints under the Window*, written in 1933, concludes in this way: "And have you guessed by this time, my readers, that the footprints under the window were those of the famous detective, Fenton Hardy?"[7] That sort of direct address was rare even at the series' outset, but long-winded summaries of previous series volumes were common narrative intrusions. Now such recapitulation has been tapered down to a quick — usually one sentence in length — reference to the penultimate title. In general, the style shift in the Hardy Boys books might be characterized as a normalization. A style that never really asserted itself, in the manner of Arthur M. Winfield in the Rover Boys series, has given way to virtually invisible writing. Raymond Chandler said of Hammett's work that it "had style, but his audience didn't know it."[8] The Hardy Boys books have no identifiable style, especially the post-1960 volumes, even when searched by a literary critic's keen private eye.

The substance of the Hardy Boys series has undergone alteration as well, regarding both the details of the boys' lives and the kind of crimes they investigate. In the tenth Hardy Boys book, *What Happened at Midnight*, published in 1931, the opening chapter contains an extended description of Bayport's newest building, an automat; in 1941, in *The Mystery of the Flying Express*, the boys are found guarding a hydrofoil; now they play and appreciate rock music. The activities of criminal characters have changed from a never-ending parade of searching for missing treasure, counterfeiting, and auto thefts to bigger stuff. While still operating from their Bayport base, the two detectives now take on, in addition to more generic cases of kidnapping or stolen objets d'art, work involving international gambling rings, purloined Pentagon documents, schemes of political overthrow, and hijacked nuclear cargo.

Nonetheless, the underlying mystery plot formulas have remained intact throughout the characters' face lifts and the renovations in the form and matter of the stories themselves. The essential ingredients of a Hardys title are fast-paced investigative action and a large dollop of the conventional gimmickry of pulp magazine detection that began with Nick Carter: disguises, ciphers to be puzzled out, rude thugs to be put in their places, crime kits, secret messages, and passwords. The thirty-ninth member of the series, *The Mystery of the Chinese Junk*, published in 1960, illustrates the basic recipe for exciting boy readers.

The two Hardys and their pals — Chet Morton, Biff Hooper, Tony Prito, and Jim Foy — decide to buy a used Chinese junk that Foy's cousin in New York City has told them about, for Bayport needs a reliable ferry service across Barmet Bay to Rocky Isle. Besides, it's June and the boys need a summer project. And as Tony says, "The junk may once have belonged to a Chinese pirate and have jade treasure hidden aboard!"[9] It will turn out, of course, that he's not far wrong.

At home, the Hardy Boys are told by their "sometimes peppery" Aunt Gertrude, who is keeping house for them while their parents are in Los Angeles, that their nationally renowned detective father has telephoned. He wants his sons to keep their eyes open for a pair of rare gold cuff links inset with a bluish amber tiger. It seems this jewelry has been smuggled into the United States from Hong Kong. Plot line number 1 has been cast out, and other matters are turned to. First, a prowler with a fearsome-looking Oriental face appears at the window of the Hardys' Elm Street home. Next, two new hundred-dollar bills, reward money the boys earned from their work on a previous case, turn up missing. Aunt Gertrude must lend them the money they will contribute to the purchase of the junk. Frank and Joe set off to New York to see the boat, though not before a confrontation with crusty Clams Daggett, who threatens the boys if they try to take business away from his own ferry service. Thus a third line of conflict and mystery has been introduced.

In New York, the boys are satisfied with the *Hai Hau* and are about to buy it when four insistent Chinese, led by one Chin Gok, attempt to purchase the boat themselves. Later, the boys are attacked on a Chinatown street by masked assailants, also Chinese; and the next morning another Chinese, George Ti-Ming, approaches them. He also wants the *Hai Hau*. When the Hardys finally get back to Bayport with their new boat, Aunt

Gertrude greets them with the news that the prowler has put in a second appearance. Things are getting so complicated the boys have to make a list:

1. Find out who the prowler is.
2. Solve the mystery behind the *Hai Hau.*
3. Learn more about Chin Gok, George Ti-Ming, and the other four Chinese.
4. Get going with our boat business! (p. 35)

The pace slackens and the suspense is leavened with humor, as Dixon gives attention to the Hardys' fat friend, Chet Morton, and his new hobby, spelunking. Then Aunt Gertrude adds yet another line of inquiry: she mentions a new and somewhat suspicious physician in town, Dr. Montrose. Determined to do some sleuthing of her own, she invites the doctor over for a visit. (It seems he makes a habit of treating widows *and* advising them on financial matters.) Meanwhile, the boys set out in the *Hai Hau.* When they call home using their shortwave equipment, a hissing voice breaks in, "Hardys, I warn you. Do not sail the *Hai Hau!*" (p. 48) Then the junk is approached by fake coastguardsmen. The crew of the *Hai Hau* shakes them, and later Frank and Joe go out in their own speedboat, the *Sleuth*, to search the bay for the impostors. Soon thereafter, another problem arises. Chet, his sister Iola, and their friend Callie Shaw have not returned from a spelunking expedition.

At this point in the book, six chapters or one-third the way along, all the plot lines have been set in motion. The remaining pages are devoted to interweaving the various narratives, building to a climactic confrontation, and eventually resolving every mystery under investigation. Chapter 7 describes the Hardys' rescue of their three chums, who blacked out in the cul de sac of a cave. The boys hop into their convertible, scour the outskirts of Bayport, and pull out Chet, Iola, and Callie in the nick of time. Hours later, Iola casually mentions, "Oh, I almost forgot! Look what I found this afternoon. It was on the ground just outside the cave" (p. 69). What she found was a gold cuff link. Further, the party of explorers had overheard men talking outside the cave about the Hardy Boys and how they were fouling up plans.

The boys phone their father to report the latest development; and when he asks them to retrieve from his wall safe a top-secret file on the notorious Chameleon thief, the file is not there. The boys decide to call in the police. Within minutes the agreeable Chief Collig and his plainclothes assistants are on the scene. (The cooperation between the Hardys and the law will come as a surprise to readers of earlier volumes in the series.) Then Frank and Joe head out to follow up another line of investigation—namely, the shady Dr. Montrose.

Concurrently, Chin Gok and George Ti-Ming resume efforts to take over the *Hai Hau*. In a suspenseful stormy night scene, four masked men attempt to kidnap Chet, but the Hardys and company come to his aid "yelling like Indians on the warpath" and fists swinging. When they finally get home, Aunt Gertrude revives them with steaming hot cocoa and chicken sandwiches. (One of her principal duties in the story is to fortify the Hardys and their friends for their sleuthing; elsewhere she feeds them flaky-crusted beef pie, roast beef and chocolate pie, strawberry shortcake, and muffins).

The clues are mounting up. Over on Rocky Isle, in another cave, the boys find a half-burned letter concerning stock shares in a mining company. The machine on which the letter was typed is traced to Dr. Montrose. At the eerie, decaying mansion where the doctor lives, Frank and Joe find another gold cuff link—one must conclude that the Hardys' foes have a hard time holding on to things. The next day Biff and Tony reveal that they have seen lights on the western cliff of Rocky Isle: somebody was sending a coded message!

The resolution of the multiple mysteries comes in the last three chapters of *The Mystery of the Chinese Junk*. It is necessarily involved, given the number of narrative threads. George Ti-Ming proves to be a private detective from Hong Kong looking for a stolen junk in which goods are being smuggled into the U.S. The phony Dr. Montrose, who turns out to be the Chameleon, takes a powder, but the Hardys and their friends trail him to the Rocky Isle cave. In a beautiful underground cavern, they come upon the smugglers' hideaway—and the Chameleon, Chin Gok, and the would-be coastguardsmen. True to character, Frank and Joe confront the hoodlums directly, and the miscreants confess, obligingly filling in all the details of their schemes. Then they attempt to throw the boys into a slime-covered pool in the cave. The tables are turned, though the Chameleon, living up to his name, climbs out of the ooze and desperately tries one last get-away. Clams Daggett, a friend after all, prevents his escape.

The final revelation in this complicated case comes when Tony Prito finds a secret panel within the glass eye on the *Hai Hau*'s figurehead. Behind the panel is a faded treasure map locating rich blue amber mines in China. George Ti-Ming gives the Hardys and their friends a 10-percent interest in the mines as their reward for unearthing the clue to the fortune. As they wave goodbye to Ti-Ming, Frank and Joe, according to convention, wonder what new mystery will turn up to challenge them. The narrator signs off with the answer: "They had no way of knowing that very soon a most unusual case, *The Mystery of the Desert Giant*, would test their sleuthing abilities to the limit."

Tony Prito, Biff Hooper, and Chet Morton have supported Frank and Joe Hardy from the series' inception. Since the period of *The Mystery of the Chinese Junk*, minority friends like Jim Foy have made guest appearances in particular titles — in *The Mysterious Caravan*, to cite another example, a Jamaican boy named William gets involved in the Hardys' detecting. Of the regulars, Chet Morton is undoubtedly the most central. As seen in *Chinese Junk*, his role exceeds that typically assigned to fat friends in Stratemeyer books. Beyond providing comic relief through his ever-shifting hobbies, his gullibility, and his indefatigable appetite, Chet is a catalyst for drawing the Hardys into dangerous and suspenseful adventure.

More often than not, Chet replaces the fair sex as the object of a daring rescue. In fact, girls play a decidedly minor role in the Hardy Boys mysteries compared with the status of friends of the opposite sex in either the Rover Boys or Ruth Fielding books. Callie Shaw has been the "object of Frank's affection" for over fifty years without undergoing any character development or appreciable change. (Her hair color has gone from brown to blonde.) Chet's sister Iola has been deemed "all right, as a girl" by Joe for an equal period. (Unlike her brother, Iola has lost weight over the years; once plump, she is now described as slender.) As a Grosset and Dunlap publicity blurb put it in the 1930s, Frank and Joe "think girls are all right — *in their place!*" That place has always been, and still is, window dressing. The only identifiable function served by females in the series is that of rewarder: they are among the first to heap praise on the Hardys' sleuthing at the end of most volumes. Two girlfriends of Callie and Iola exclaim over the boys at the end of *The Shore Road Mystery*:

> "They are sure a pair of heroes," said Paula Robinson.
> "I really think they ought to be in a book," added Tessie, her twin.[10]

The Hardys and their circle of assistants and well-wishers are high school students, *but* they tackle grown-up crimes, which are usually supplied by their eminent criminologist father. Accordingly, the boys must be ready to fight serious criminal opposition — with their fists, with weapons, with investigative know-how. In *Chinese Junk* they have memorized the serial numbers of the one-hundred-dollar bills that are stolen from their father's safe and so are able to recognize the currency later; they set up a fairly elaborate alarm system at their house; they can "read" footprints. In time, their fame as able investigators spreads. Even as late as 1943, in *The Flickering Torch Mystery*, the junior Hardys must tactfully offer their services to clients who actually sought Fenton Hardy's aid, but these days dad seems miffed when the world doesn't know about his boys' talent: "I'm surprised you haven't heard of the fine work my sons have done," he tells a university president in *Game Plan for Disaster*.[11] Last of all, the two Hardys receive substantial monetary rewards for their detective work — how better to underscore its professional quality?[12]

In Franklin W. Dixon's series the adversaries are new in each book — no Josiah Crabtrees to be kicked around decade in and decade out, as was the case in the Rover Boys fiction. The names of the Hardys' villains sound like those belonging to the felons in the *Dick Tracy* comic strip, which, in fact, began four years after the inception of the Hardy Boys: Mortimer Prince, Baldy Turk, Meeb and Scrabby, Vordo Bleeker, Baby Face, and — in *Chinese Junk* — the Chameleon. These names not only identify the bearers irrefutably as the evildoers, but I think they are also meant to suggest the tough, big-league nature of the cases the Hardys get involved in. No local foes here; Bayport's nasty citizens, like Clams Daggett, invariably turn out to be red herrings. This is not to say that world-class thugs do not carry on their activities in Bayport. As the Chameleon shows, they do — and with phenomenal regularity. A small New England coastal town, Bayport nonetheless holds a magnetic attraction for smugglers, robbers, and extortionists, due no doubt in large part to Fenton Hardy's practice there. Thus, as often as the heroes visit locales like Africa, Mexico, or the Bahamas in the course of their work, big-time crime comes to them in Bayport.

The interaction and conflict between detectives and their opposition is as codified as the characters involved. Arthur Prager suggests that Hardy Boys mystery plots follow a four-part formula.[13] First, Fenton Hardy "hands down" a case. (Alternatively, his sons spot a suspicious character in Bayport.) Second, there is the fortuitous coincidence: the Hardys overhear suspects plotting or spy a potential criminal in a compromising position. Third, trouble develops when the boys follow the trail left by the evildoers. Typically, dirty tricks are enacted against the young detectives, and sometimes these pranks are intentionally deadly: the Chameleon plans to drown the boys in that cavern pool. Fourth, there is the final chapter. Having tumbled into their foes' clutches, the Hardys are miraculously rescued at the eleventh hour. In the meantime, the villains have confessed everything. My synopsis of Prager's formulas does provide an accurate description of the scripts in most Hardy Boys novels, though there are variant formulas — for example, in *The Mystery of the Spiral Bridge*, it is Fenton Hardy who is kidnapped while he is investigating sabotage of a road-building project in Kentucky.[14] But beyond the outlined formulas, something need be said about the degree of multiple plotting that has become a Franklin W. Dixon trademark. *The Mystery of the Chinese Junk* offers five different mysteries to be unraveled. What keeps readers guessing, moreover, is not so much the outcome of each as the interconnection that will inevitably tie together the disparate threads. The final exposition of the plot(s) is generally lengthy in a Hardy Boys story, as it must be given the number of lines of action and inquiry, and it is ritualistically celebrated by a family reunion, a dance, or, most frequently, a banquet.

Occasionally, the detection in the Hardy Boys books is heightened by an atmosphere of horror, as in *The Case of the Screeching Owl, The Witchmaster's Key,* and *Night of the Werewolf.* And in the 1960s and 1970s the Hardys mysteries come close to earning the designation "spy fiction." *Secret Agent on Flight 101, The Arctic Patrol Mystery* (involving a plot on a U.S. astronaut's life), and *The Pentagon Spy* (concerning the theft of top-secret government documents) — these titles are suspenseful tales of international espionage. As a rule, however, the Hardy Boys series books are without Gothic or espionage embellishments. Their method is straightforward detection, detection accomplished not through deduction but by the search, or chase. At the end of the first series volumes, Grosset and Dunlap ran advertisements, one of which asked this question: "Have You Ever Thought Why You Get So Much Fun Out of Reading the Hardy Boys Stories?" The supplied answer does indeed pinpoint the books' basic attraction:

> It's probably because the Hardy Boys, Joe and Frank, are fellows like yourself. They like action, plenty of it. They are as full of curiosity as a couple of bloodhounds. And just leave a mystery around and they'll be in it before you can say "Sherlock Holmes!"
>   . . .
> It's because they can drive a car and pilot a speedboat and are at home in the great outdoors and keep their heads in an emergency (and an emergency always is just around the corner).

In short, the Stratemeyer Syndicate in the Hardy Boys series had settled on a whirlwind mixture of mystery and adventure that spelled popularity with young readers.

When Tony Prito hypothesized that the junk may have belonged to a Chinese pirate and may contain hidden jade treasure, he is participating in everyboy's fantasy adventure, the fantasy that explains in large part the thrill the fast-paced adventure genre has held for boys since the days of *Robinson Crusoe, The Coral Island,* and *Treasure Island.* The secret the Stratemeyer Syndicate hit upon in the Hardy Boys books was the *packing* of timeless adventure-story action into a distinctive, and repeatable, detective fiction pattern. Thus, the novel lure of the detective mystery had at last been thoroughly fused with the earlier adventure tale tradition. In this respect, the Hardys do pick up where the Rovers left off. That older set of brothers, from time to time, hunted treasure and sailed the seas as part of some larger investigation, as in *The Rover Boys Down East*; Frank and Joe make a habit of it.

The Hardys' bayside location leads to numerous expeditions in the *Sleuth*, and other seaside mysteries come along, too—such as *The Phantom Freighter* and *Trapped at Sea.* On or off the water, the Hardys' detection is likely to incorporate some "digging" for hidden treasure, as series titles make clear (*The Tower Treasure, Hunting for Hidden Gold, The Melted Coins, The Secret of Pirate's Hill, The Mystery of Smuggler's Cove*, and others). In fact, the unearthing of treasure is one of the most common climactic moments in Hardy Boys books, the staple ingredient that comes just before the boys fall into the hands of the evil characters, according to the basic plot formula. Frank and Joe's searches for secret goods are, to be sure, more elaborate than the expedition made in a simple tale of treasure hunting. Like Jim Hawkins in *Treasure Island*, the boys must first penetrate the criminal rings who are also after, or have stolen, precious objects, gold, or valuable papers. Hence, they are involved in two activities central to the active (versus the cerebral or contemplative) strain of detective fiction: they spy and they eavesdrop on their opponents. Both these practices are exciting to readers for the very reason that they are secretive endeavors, visual or aural as the case may be.

Where do the Hardy Boys carry out their searches? In archetypal secret places, namely deserted islands, caves, and underground tunnels. *Chinese Junk* makes use of all three hideaways; other titles are self-descriptive—*The Secret of the Caves, The Mystery of Cabin Island, The Secret of the Lost Tunnel.* Islands have long been part of boys' adventure fiction, in part because they are by their very nature set off from the rest of civilization and are often terra incognita, the equivalent of the untamed frontier in western adventure stories. Islands, what is more, according to C. G. Jung, are figures for the self, and explorations of the self, or searches for identity, constitute the major theme in adolescent litera- ture.[15] Caves and concomitant underground tunnels and passage- ways are secret places by definition. Psychoanalyst Lili Peller has commented that stories about uncovering secrets are naturals for children, for whom life is full of secrets adults are guarding.[16] More specifically, Prager has suggested a Freudian fascination in the Hardy Boys series with yawning-mouthed caves.[17] It is true that Bayport has an extremely developed system of labyrin- thine caverns and passageways, in which stolen goods have in- evitably been secreted. But in their use of islands and caves the creators of the Hardy Boys fiction are consciously following not Freud but the example set by nineteenth-century writers of boys' adventure books. And the Stratemeyer Syndicate was not alone in keeping the tradition alive within a new mystery format. One of the children's books reviewed in the pages of the *Saturday Review* for 1935 was S. S. Smith's *The Cave Mystery*, the story of two Spanish boys who investigate caves in the Basque Pyrenees.[18]

The Hardy Boys series resembles contemporary detective fiction for adults in its blend of adventure and mystery. As pointed out in earlier chapters, the American hard-boiled mystery has its roots in the romantic western adventure story. Speaking of this mix, George Grella notes, "the American detective novel, paradoxically, combines its romance themes [good triumphing over evil] and structures with a tough, realistic surface and a highly sensational content."[19] Now the Hardy Boys books also mix romantic adventure plots with a superficial realism, be it the advent of the automat or the boys' love for fast transportation. And the series displays a criminal content sufficiently sensation- al — viz., armed culprits intent on doing the boys in — to have trig- gered alarm among librarians and educators. But there is a great difference between the "mean streets" of the adult genre, where murder comes cheap and the entire world is stained by corrup- tion, and the crime-ridden though ultimately comfortable and serene world of Bayport. The social context in which Frank and Joe Hardy operate and the underlying world view in the novels keep them firmly in the realm of the adventure *fantasy*.

Raymond Chandler said of the milieu in American novels of

detection, "It is not a fragrant world." Inordinate criminal activity notwithstanding, Bayport smells sweet. It is indeed a rarefied, almost fantastic place, constructed from much the same mold as the Dodge or Cheyenne of western fiction, where outlaws rode into town but were always put behind bars before the story ended. While lawbreakers from around the world intrude upon Bayport and the Hardys sometimes must travel far to apprehend their prey, the halcyon moral climate and golden rules operative in Bayport forever obtain. The Hardys always get their man, and in the wide world people and circumstances bend to the boys' needs as surely as they do at home. The dust jackets of the most recent Hardy Boys volumes sum up the prevailing opinion in the Hardys' universe: "Believing that right will triumph — that lawbreakers can be brought to justice — the Hardys work day and night to accomplish their ends." Their outlook, as well as their adversaries, can be likened to Dick Tracy's.

The Bayport citizenry back their famous young detectives wholeheartedly. The town's Automobile Club, for example, holds a banquet in the Hardys' honor after they bust open a car theft ring in *The Shore Road Mystery*; and by the era of *Chinese Junk* official lawmen work with the boys eagerly, to the point of obsequiousness. (At first, the law was presented as something of an obstacle, due to Irish cops' thickheadedness.) Significantly, the Bayport adults also stay in the background of Dixon's books. This is particularly true of Laura and Fenton Hardy. The boys' pretty mother might as well be absent from the scene, for she is a shadowy figure who emerges only to smile proudly after her boys have cracked a case. Their father provides the fodder for their sleuthing appetites — and then he conveniently leaves town to work on another case, which always turns out to be integrally related to what his sons are investigating. The senior Hardy's peripheral presence is also useful in setting the tone of detection in the books. He reminds readers that the boys are not just playing at being private eyes: they are working on their father's important cases, though Fenton at times seems almost laughable with his large assortment of detective paraphernalia. "Taking any disguises, Dad?" Joe asks as his father sets off on a case.[20] The boy refers to Mr. Hardy's vast assortment of costumes, masks, and wigs used for the purpose of impersonation. Finally, there is Aunt Gertrude, seemingly a deterrent to the boys' fun and independence. She frequently keeps house for the boys while their parents are away and, despite her much-made-of irascibility, is a pushover for the boys.

At bottom, Bayport is not a place that fires readers' imaginations, as settings so often do in literature for the young, be they realistic or fantastic places. Since Franklin W. Dixon is a cardboard writer, it is, of course, understandable that Bayport remains only a formulaic backdrop, as forgettable as the settings in soap operas or 1950s television situation comedies. Bayport is in fact reminiscent of a place like Springfield in *Father Knows Best*. It's there for characters to live in, it is secure, it throws up no real dilemmas — and Bayport is an especially handy place for the Hardys to be since so many criminals flock there. But it is not a spot that takes on its own life. In short, it is *not* Sherwood Anderson's Winesburg, Ohio (who would expect it to be?); it is not even as full-bodied as the Tutter, Illinois, of the contemporary Jerry Todd books for boys.[21] It is a frozen and fixed world where mysteries come and go, but there is no change or human complexity.

Eudora Welty has observed, "Place . . . has the most delicate control over character . . . by confining character, it defines it."[22] And so Bayport does. So different from the messy, unfragrant world depicted relentlessly in hard-boiled detective fiction, Bayport superficially looks like a real place but is actually a fantasy island. The Hardys, in turn, are frozen characters in ways that preceding Stratemeyer stars like Ruth Fielding and even the Rovers were not.

In point of fact, the Hardy Boys have aged two years apiece in the development of the series. Frank was sixteen and Joe fifteen in the beginning; by the 1960s Frank has turned eighteen, Joe seventeen. This detail aside, the boys are for all intents and purposes as suspended in time as they are firmly rooted — at least mentally — in place. The series and its heroes are static; the two sets of Rover Boys books were open-ended, protean by comparison. In Dixon's oeuvre, the characters do exactly the same things year after year. They find another cave to explore, another international smuggling ring to smash open. In short, the Hardys remain locked in that period between childhood and adult life that psychologist Erik Erikson has characterized as a moratorium — the quiet and deep sleep of fairy tale characters that precedes awakening into maturity.[23] In their perpetual moratorium, they keep reenacting the same patterns, keep solving cases for the fun of it. As one former fan put it, "the Hardy Boys were left behind. . . . The logical conclusion is that [they] are dead, or at least moribund, locked in their antique Bayport, doomed to chase the same diamond smugglers in the same roadster until diamonds are obsolete and nobody cares."[24] Frank and Joe bring to mind the dark side of Peter Pan's charmed existence as an eternal boy. Where the Rovers exemplify the fun of not being a grown-up, the Hardys recall the restrictions or constraints of such a fate. Peter is, finally, arrested by his confinement on the island of Neverland; unlike the other lost boys, he cannot choose to go back to London and grow up. Realizing this, Peter "wailed piteously" in his nightmares.[25] Luckily for them, the Hardy Boys are not cursed with the power of reflection.

The dark statements above reflect my adult reaction to reading and rereading books in a series of eighty titles. They are the reflections of one who has tried to go back to a pleasant playground of youth but failed to rekindle the excitement. As James Barrie, the creator of Neverland, said of his imaginary landscape: "On these magic shores, children at play are for ever beaching their coracles. We too have been there; we can still hear the sound of the surf, though we shall land no more" (p. 7). But what about the Hardy Boys' fervent juvenile readership? First, and most obviously, it changes. The same boys (and girls) have not been buying the books since 1927. Approximately three and one-half generations of readers have come and gone since that date. Boys in the 1980s do indeed have more titles to choose from than did their predecessors, but it is doubtful that many consume more than half the available volumes. (They do consume a goodly number, however, as penciled interpolations in library copies of the books attest — I counted thirty-two X's on a list of the series titles at the front of one volume.) Readers grow up and out of the Hardy Boys before there is time to read each one.

There is, what is more, evidence that the average age of readers of both the Hardy Boys and Nancy Drew is declining.

Frank and Joe Hardy have grown a little older; their readers are getting younger. I have found no record of the age group originally projected by the founders of the series, but early to mid-teens is my educated guess. One reader from an earlier generation, John Gardner, has commented on how he outgrew the Hardys, "Dickens I ran into when I was in my early teens, when I began to find the Hardy boys tiresome and unconvincing. . . . The irrealism of two boys having long conversations while riding on motorcycles . . . was more than I could put up with." And in 1932 a writer for *Publishers Weekly* asserted that "publishers today recognize as a fact that boys, of their own accord, stop reading the modern juvenile series two years earlier than their fathers stopped the series of a generation ago."[26] By the era of *The Mystery of the Chinese Junk*, the Syndicate clearly conceived of the Hardys as appealing to ten- to fourteen-year-olds. The back covers of 1960s books say so: "Anyone from 10 to 14 who likes lively adventure stories, packed with mystery and action, will want to read every one of the Hardy Boys stories listed here." In recent years the age level has dropped again: the Simon and Schuster publicity advertises the series as appealing to ages eight to twelve, and membership in the Fan Club run by that publisher bears out these figures.[27]

The implications of a decline in the average age of Hardys' readers are interesting. For one thing, the age drop suggests that while the Hardy Boys' weltanschauung has not changed much over time, the society in which readers live has, with the result that children grow up faster.[28] Hence they come to and leave series such as this one earlier on in their lives than did their fathers. Most literature for 1980s adolescents is a far cry from the neat mysteries of the Hardy Boys: the problems of Chandler's mean streets are most definitely addressed in today's "Young Adult" books that are part of the publishing trend labeled "contemporary realism." The mysteries within this line of literature are closer relatives of Chandler's works in their shared view of a stained world than they are of the safe capers penned by Dixon.[29] Thus the Hardy Boys series has been pushed back to the preteen reader who has always delighted in the good adventure fantasy.

Until readers emerge from their own period of moratorium,

the Hardy Boys can exert a powerful influence, and some of the very aspects of the novels criticized above explain why — for example, the ordinariness of Bayport. The boys, too, are, paradoxically, average guys, "fellows like youself" as the publicity went, even as they perform wondrous feats of detection. They can be likened to Wally and The Beaver or David and Ricky Nelson of the TV sitcoms, rather than the superlative Rovers, who were always at the head of their class.[30] Average fellows from a town that is depicted as a quaint Everytown, U.S.A., right down to the smiling policemen and helpful shopkeepers. But *these* ordinary boys get mixed up in high-level detection and dangerous adventure.

This fantasy scenario offers readers more than escapist thrills. Like the fairy tales, it provides a story in which the young and relatively inexperienced triumph; consequently, it gives an encouraging, confidence-inspiring model for life.[31] Further, the security of the Hardys' existence (though always in danger, they are never seriously harmed) offers comfort as well from the anxieties brought on by the biological and psychological pressures of growing up in a world that most likely resembles Bayport and its extended universe but little. Readers need to spend quiet hours in such a retreat — in a moratorium, if you will — during which they can amass latent energy for the last stage of growth into adulthood. The readily available, jam-packed, and familiar mystery adventures of Frank and Joe Hardy fill that time slot to a T

Nancy signaled frantically for help.

—The Clue of the Tapping Heels
Carolyn Keene
Grosset and Dunlap, 1939

6

NANCY DREW
Gothic Detection

"If you keep on the way you've started, you'll surely edge your old dad out of his practice yet," said Mr. Drew.

Nancy gave her father's arm an affectionate pinch.

. . .

"I'm beginning to think it may be wise to protect my practice by taking you in as a partner."

Nancy smiled, highly flattered at the praise her father had bestowed upon her.

"All right," she declared eagerly. "Put out your sign. 'Carson Drew and Daughter.'"

— *The Secret at Shadow Ranch*

Carson Drew expressed the sentiments above in the fifth volume of the Nancy Drew series, written in 1930, the year Carolyn Keene introduced her blonde, teenage sleuth nonpareil. For over half a century Nancy has averaged almost 1.5 cases per year, and at present some two or three titles are issued annually.[1] While never accorded official partnership in her dad's law practice, she has handled many investigative assignments for him over the years, as well as much work she has taken on herself. The cases she has cracked, it must be acknowledged, have not always matched the detecting coups of the Hardy Boys in scope. A far greater proportion concern missing antiques, stolen jewels, and false claims to inheritance in or near her hometown of River Heights, rather than the practices of international crooks — though especial-

ly since the 1960s Nancy Drew has turned to extensive traveling and run into assorted smugglers, kidnappers, and other evildoers along the way. Like Ruth Fielding, Nancy can never get
away from it all; a mystery lurks at the destination of every pleasure trip.

The girl's achievements are in no way diminished by the fact
that most of her detection is done locally. Indeed, she is a legend
in her own time in the world within her series. It is the rule that
new acquaintances have read of her exploits in their newspaper.
"You are often spoken of in glowing terms for your cleverness
in apprehending unscrupulous people," a potential client comments.[2] Concerning breadth of achievements, this Syndicate heroine is omnitalented. In the last fifty-five years she has displayed
a knack for about everything — from piloting planes and boats
to swimming and shooting game, from acting and dancing to
evaluating art and writing short stories. Who else could tap dance
in Morse code? What other fictional hero or heroine has ever
maneuvered a car so skillfully? Her analytical skills are keen, too.
She deciphers codes, old manuscripts, and ancient inscriptions
with dispatch; in Nancy Drew the Stratemeyer Syndicate finally came up with a detective who combines deduction with quick
legwork and amazing intuitive abilities. She thinks rings around
the sometimes dimwitted Hardys.

According to current Syndicate records, upward to eighty
million copies of the Nancy Drew books have been sold; two and
a half million paperbacks have been purchased in the last three
years.[3] The back endpaper of every library edition of the series
I have checked out is covered with stamped due dates.[4] Another
measure of the series' success is that among all American girls
series books Nancy Drew has received the lion's share of critical
attention. As this chapter should make clear, she has been featured in every existing book-length study of the series book
phenomenon. Articles about Carolyn Keene and her creation
have appeared in scholarly journals, *The Wall Street Journal*, *Vogue*
and *Ms.* magazines; a poem bearing Nancy's name has been
published in *Poetry*; and prominent essayists like Ellen Goodman
and Frances Fitzgerald have written about the teen detective's
significance. Still another sign of her impact is the fact that the
figure of the teenage female sleuth, informed in large part by the
character of Nancy Drew, has been the butt of satiric films and

plays. (Just last week I learned of a local theater's upcoming offering of *Trixie True, Teen Detective.*)

Nancy may be the teen detective queen, but there are many attendants in her court. Among Stratemeyer offerings in the 1920s, at least four heroines spent a good amount of their energy solving mysteries: Ruth Fielding, Billie Bradley, Betty Gordon, and Nan Sherwood. Another series — the Blythe Girls begun in 1925 — though more a member of the sentimental romance genre frequently contained mystery subplots and introduced a figure named Chester Drew, who in name anyhow may have inspired Keene's Carson Drew.[5] And after Nancy Drew a long line of girl gumshoes followed, both in and outside the Syndicate: the Dana Girls, Judy Bolton, Trixie Belden, Cherry Ames, and Kay Tracey, to name only some of the most prominent.[6] In England, Sylvia Silence aided her eccentric investigator father as early as 1922 in the story paper *Schoolgirls' Weekly*, and approximately a decade later, in 1933, Sylvia's creator, John W. Bobin, invented another girl detective by the name interestingly enough of Valerie Drew.[7] This flourishing tradition set forth, the facts remain that Nancy Drew was the first major full-time investigator in American girls' series books and that she has displayed inimitable lasting power.

Nancy has outlasted the foremost authors of her series. Conceived by Edward Stratemeyer, who wrote the first three titles in the series just before he died (*The Secret of the Old Clock, The Hidden Staircase*, and *The Bungalow Mystery*), Nancy was then inherited by Stratemeyer's daughter Harriet Stratemeyer Adams, who once said she came to regard Nancy as her "fiction daughter." Immediately, Adams made some changes in the Syndicate's budding star. "She had been too bold and too bossy," according to Adams, and this author accordingly altered Nancy's treatment of Hannah Gruen, the Drews' housekeeper.[8] Adams elsewhere confirmed that what she calls "half-ghosts" — writers who filled in plot outlines but were in no way responsible for story ideas — have been involved in the series attributed to Carolyn Keene.[9] When she died in 1982, the current Syndicate partners were left with the responsibility of continuing the Drew saga. Today Nancy Axelrad keeps the young detective going, and the Bobbsey Twins as well.

What are the secrets of the Nancy Drew mysteries? First,

surface changes have been made to keep the series abreast of new generations' tastes in fashions, automobiles, and fun. The dust jackets and, more recently, the cover art have been changed many times, as have illustrations within the books. Initially, Nancy was neatly dressed in a blue traveling suit and white gloves; she wore pastel frocks to afternoon teas and fraternity parties; her hair style was a "curly golden bob." By 1935, the bob was intact, but Nancy was pictured on the dust jacket of *The Secret of the Hollow Oak* in a longish brown walking skirt and sporty jacket. In the 1960s Nancy could be found in shirtwaist dresses, and her hair had become "titian-colored." Now she wears jeans, but only for the more physical aspects of her detecting; usually she works in the kinds of casual skirts and blouses seen in "Junior Miss" sections of department stores. Her hair has inexplicably inched back toward the blonde ("strawberry" is the usual adjective).

These emendations, though, have far less to do with Nancy Drew's longevity than do the constant features of the series — namely, the mixture of active and suspenseful exploration of some unknown criminal scheme and the strong Gothic undercurrent that aligns these novels with that genre of horrific fiction that began with Ann Radcliffe's *The Mysteries of Udolpho*. Let's consider *The Clue in the Crumbling Wall*.

In chapter 1 Nancy is faced with two assaults: her purse containing a potentially valuable pearl she discovered in a local river clam is stolen, and her garden has been violated — painted daisies and hollyhocks trampled and four choice rose bushes removed. Almost instantaneously, Lieutenant Masters, a young policewoman described in the terms reserved for good characters in the series ("charming," "cultured," etc.) appears and tracks down the garden saboteur, an eight-year-old named Joan Fenimore.

The first complication in the plot has been arrived at. Joan and her poor mother are eking out an existence, but they live in the shadow of a family mystery. Mrs. Fenimore's sister, Florianna "Flossie" Johnson, was a talented and famous dancer until she disappeared while on a vacation trip, an odd occurrence since she was newly engaged to a wealthy manufacturer named Walter Heath. Heath died five years after Flossie's disappearance and left his estate, including Heath Castle, a mansion in the English style, to his missing betrothed. Now—in exactly three weeks, to be precise—this unclaimed inheritance is to be converted into a county park. This case is made to order for Nancy Drew, who specializes in bringing or restoring wealth to its rightful claimants, and the added time factor in the mystery increases its challenge. Mrs. Fenimore asks the girl to help her and her daughter establish their claim to the fortune, for she like "nearly everyone in River Heights . . . knew that [Nancy] was as clever as she was pretty."[10] Nancy demurs at first—"I hardly know what to say," she says—but naturally accepts the invitation.

Walter Heath had made his fortune in buttons: he had a button factory on his estate, which used the fresh water mussels from the Muskoka River. The entire estate, Nancy learns, is presently being looked after by a shady lawyer with the giveaway name of Hector Keep. The young investigator asks her ever-ready chums, George Fayne and Bess Marvin, to take a motor-boat ride with her up the Muskoka to explore the estate. Out on the water, hapless Bess immediately topples into the water when another boat collides with them. Nancy must dive in and rescue her. Never one to take a hint that somebody does not want her interference, Nancy goes back to the castle by car. This time she and George meet with an explosion. Typical of the chain of difficulties the detective gets into, she is hurled by the blast into a storage closet, the door slams shut, and the ceiling caves in.

At home meanwhile, her father, renowned lawyer Carson Drew, displays a rare nervous reaction to Nancy's activities, though he says he knows it is useless to ask his determined daughter to give up the case. (He's right.) Instead, he agrees to accompany her to Heath Castle—she has by now extricated herself from the closet—and there they find two clues: "freshly made footprints" (a staple of a Nancy Drew mystery) and a torn scrap of paper on which are the remnants of a note,

Dear C,
    Some
cret which I
in a wall
famous
worthy
    (p. 64)

Housekeeper Hannah Gruen later makes the helpful suggestion that Nancy check the handwriting of the note against Walter Heath's signature on books he has given to the River Heights Historical Society. Hannah seems to have a special interest in this organization, for in the 1980s she continues to urge Nancy to research her cases in their archives.[11]

Next, Nancy decides to return to the castle-cum-button factory, this time by plane; the place apparently draws her magnetically. Nancy, Carolyn Keene interjects, feels every girl should learn to fly. At this point in the story faithful readers' inevitable question — where is Nancy's boyfriend Ned Nickerson? — is answered. He is off in South America, and Nancy's pulse quickens at the sight of a letter he has sent her. It is thus established that George and Bess will serve as Nancy's only sidekicks on this case. Once again, the three head out to Heath Castle for a picnic in the "Faerie Gallerie." Now it is George who falls into the water; she wanders off and plummets into a stagnant pool choked with water lilies. Her clothes, which she has set out to dry in the sun, are mysteriously stolen by a twelve-year-old boy in a scene that illustrates the extent of the sexual content in the series. On another part of the estate, Nancy has slipped through an open side door into the castle itself. She hears a cry and frantically searches through the dark rooms full of sheet-draped furniture; she thinks Flossie Johnson may be imprisoned, in the tower most likely. "How like olden times to imprison someone in a tower!" she remarks heavyhandedly (p. 84). Readers know that her turn is coming as she ascends the circular iron stairway to the tower room.

Sure enough, somebody locks Nancy in, and even she is unable to negotiate the forty-foot drop from the parapet to the ground. Nor can she pry open the door lock with her nail file. Just as she begins to feel faint, a stranger clandestinely helps her to escape. At home once more, she tells her father that the castle walls are not crumbling from age: they are being tampered with for some purpose.

Pursuing another angle of the case, Nancy sets out to discover what became of Flossie Johnson. In nearby Hampton she locates an immensely forthcoming tourist-home owner whose memory is long. The woman will certainly help the young sleuth, who's "hardly a stranger by name," for her exploits have been covered by the local paper. The gist of the informant's story is this: the dancer had come to the tourist home ten years before to recover after being hit by an automobile. The owner further remembers that Miss Johnson had mentioned something about a farm near Plainville.

Nancy and her assistants turn to deciphering the partial note found earlier at Heath Castle. In an uncharacteristic burst of insight, Bess comes up with a hypothetical completion. Walter Heath, she concludes, has hidden in the wall a "worthy secret" that will make him famous. But it is Nancy who knows where to find the gloss for the cryptic message. She retrieves a book on old houses and gardens, in which there happens to be an illustrated discussion of the original on which Walter Heath's mansion was based. This book contains the essential clue:

> It was a quotation in Old English. . . . Nancy, who had learned
> to read the works of the old English poet Chaucer in school,
> eagerly translated it.
>   "'I have hid my treasures in the niches of the cloister
> through which, all unsuspecting, the gay men and fair ladies
> pass each day to bathe,'" she read. (p. 130)

Never mind that Chaucer wrote in *Middle* English, Nancy knows how to interpret a clue when she finds one: she is certain there is treasure to be found in a cloister within the Heath Castle gardens.

There is — in the form of a rusty metal box buried in the wall. In the box Nancy discovers a journal that mentions a process for extracting magenta dye from the whelk shells Heath used in making buttons. This must be the "worthy secret" referred to in the torn scrap of note. There is yet another clue in the wall as well, a cement block containing a picture of a woman's slipper and the inscription "Cinderella." A specialist in footprints, Nancy guesses that Flossie Johnson's foot will fit this slipper and that the lost dancer is no doubt the "C" addressed in the note. The evidence is mounting up nicely, but a problem remains. A sinister figure approaches, "walking with a catlike tread along the flagstone cloister" (p. 157). It is Hector Keep!

Nancy and her friends escape pell mell, and that concludes the hair-raising part of the story. The last sixty pages of *The Clue in the Crumbling Wall* are devoted to unraveling the cat's cradle of intersecting narrative threads. A strange woman appears and asserts that she is Flossie Johnson. She produces the other half of the message the girls had found and stakes her claim to the Heath fortune, but the impostor is quickly exposed by Nancy. (Her feet were too big to fit the slipper mold in the wall.) Then the sleuth tracks down the real Florianna in a dungeon at the castle. This "beautiful character with great charm" had been kidnapped and confined by Hector Keep and his minions, who were searching for the formula for the magenta dye themselves, in addition to seeing to it that the fiancée of Heath did not return to ask for her rightful inheritance. Finally, readers are given to believe that Flossie, her sister, and little Joan will live happily thereafter, thanks to the tireless sleuthing of Nancy Drew.

The formulas of characterization and plotting in Carolyn Keene's series differ but little from those at work in the Hardy Boys books. The villains go by names like Hector Keep, Bushy Trott, Alpha Zinn, Tom Tozzle, Fred Bunce, or Felix Raybolt. Once in a while there is a villainess—for example, Mrs. Dondo in *The Hidden Window Mystery*. As usual in Stratemeyer titles, their names give away their status, and so do their nonstandard grammar, their rough and impolite behavior, and—especially in this series—their clothing. As Nancy's wardrobe has followed vicissitudes of fashion, the antagonists' have, too. But the latter always overdo it when it comes to apparel, whether their sartorial preference runs toward flashy checked suits, showy ensembles that are unsuited for afternoon wear (among the women), or, more recently, "trendy" designer jeans and a fisherman's knit sweater. Good characters, by contrast, like Lieutenant Masters in *Crumbling Wall* are decorous in taste, speak in rich, modulated tones, and rush immediately to Nancy's assistance. The assignment of characters to either stereotypically bad or equally good status is even more pronounced in this series than in earlier Stratemeyer publications. Not only do readers know forthwith which camp a character belongs to according to the signs named above, but the discerning Miss Drew intuitively evaluates every character she comes across. When, for instance, she meets two circus performers in *The Mystery of the Ivory Charm*, her judgment snaps into action. She tells her friends, "I was amazed when Rai called Coya his son. . . . Somehow Coya seems of much finer quality."[12]

Here is a shorthand summary of the standard pattern of action between Nancy Drew and those set on doing wrong. She either takes a case (sometimes it is passed on to her by her father, other times influential clients such as museum directors or wealthy dowagers actually solicit *her* help) or else she stumbles onto one, as in *Crumbling Wall*, in the first few pages of the book. More likely, both formulas are used, and as in the Hardy Boys the denouement of the story will reveal the seemingly disparate mysteries to be two sides of one puzzle. Nancy next rushes into investigation; inevitably the bad characters threaten her or try to bully her into dropping her inquiries. As Carson Drew notes time and again, however, it is no use trying to deter his daughter once she has sniffed a mystery.

The villains nonetheless keep trying. Perhaps the salient formula in a Nancy Drew book is the chain of assaults made upon the sleuth's person. It is amazing that any thinking power is left after the beatings she has taken. People are forever trying to get at her through her car, of course. The brakes and steering of the various blue models she has driven — from her first roadster to a convertible to the sports car she spins around in these days — are the most frequent targets for those wanting to get rid of the girl. Nancy, moreover, has had a snake coil around her, was nearly electrocuted by a wired puppet, has recently been struck by a clanking armored figure, and was once poisoned by a sword doll, to mention just a few of the exotic things that have happened to her. Then there are routine events like being imprisoned in some nook or cranny of a large house. (Alternatively, she is spirited away by boat and held captive in its claustrophobic cabin, as in *The Clue of the Tapping Heels*.)

Undaunted, the heroine springs back for further battering, always bolstered by the clues she finds. In point of fact, they almost find her, deus ex machina fashion. As other commentators have noted, clues are essential to the suspense and the seductiveness of the Nancy Drew series.[13] They function like the mag-

ical objects come upon by fairy-tale protagonists. They give the
plot a forward motion, or sense of progress, that is much needed
since revelation of the young detective's evolving analysis is not
a part of the series mystery modus operandi. If the detective finds
a clue, in other words, readers can assume headway is being
made in solving the case. What constitutes a clue? Generally,
it is something old, something valuable, something that exudes
special meaning or evokes sentiment — again, something almost
magical in its aura. A short list of Nancy Drew titles illustrates
the sort of clue Keene favors: *The Clue in the Diary, The Sign of
the Twisted Candles, The Mystery of the Brass Bound Trunk, The Quest
of the Missing Map, The Clue of the Black Keys, The Clue of the Velvet
Mask, The Scarlet Slipper Mystery, The Clue of the Whistling Bag-
pipes.*

Nancy perseveres, in both rebounding from her knocks and
following out her clues, and finally she uncovers the perpetrators
of evil and restores missing objects, and harmony, to those who
called upon her for assistance. Once she tracks down the thieves,
or kidnappers or smugglers, the plot is fait accompli. Things fall
into place like clockwork, due primarily to the fact that the bad
characters are suddenly overcome by the inclination to be cooperative. Not since Dan Baxter melted before the Rover Boys have
adversaries been so accommodating. "Felix Raybolt . . . what
are you doing here?" Nancy demands, and it is not long before
she breaks him down and, further, persuades the crook to write
out checks to those he has swindled.[14]

In the end, Nancy Drew acts in uncommonly modest fashion, often blushing at the praise of all who have watched her
work. Then she accepts a reward, usually in the form of some
artifact that earlier served either as a clue or the object of her
detection (or a cameo ring, a valuable doll, an old clock, a Paul
Revere bell). She does *not* accept money, as did the Hardy Boys,
but her well-established fame is a perquisite she can't deny.

Beyond her infallible ability to judge character and reduce crooks
to jelly, Nancy's defining qualities are her coolness and her independence. She never loses her composure in the face of crisis.
Caught in a dark and watery tunnel in *The Secret of the Forgotten
City*, Nancy does not panic even though she "knew she was in
serious trouble."[15] In *The Message in the Hollow Oak* she has the

presence of mind to rescue a sleepwalking friend, who meandered out onto the fire escape of their hotel, using the rope tricks learned earlier in the novel. Likewise the sleuth's calm practicality manifests itself in her reaction to the uncanny. In over seventy volumes she has been involved in an untold number of spooky confrontations, but never for a moment does she give in to the possibility that supernatural forces — forces she cannot triumph over — might be in operation. Eminently pragmatic, she pooh-poohs the fears and "overactive" imaginations of those around her. In *The Ghost of Blackwood Hall*, readers are told that Nancy "took no stock in ghosts or spirits."[16] Elsewhere she proves the point. Searching an empty house on a night when the wind whispers dismally through the swaying boughs and loose shutters creak on their rusty hinges, the girl detective runs headlong into a skeleton, whose long, bony fingers brush against her throat. Her reaction: "It's — it's nothing. Nothing but a skeleton."[17]

The ultimate effect of such sangfroid is to make Nancy Drew seem less — or more, possibly — than human. She is the premier example of what Arthur Svenson was talking about when he spoke of the Syndicate's "*Übermenschen*."[18] Even her most loyal readers have recognized that such coolheadedness, combined as it is in this heroine with easy mastery of every activity and area of study she takes up, borders at times on the ludicrous. Bobbie Ann Mason has persuasively argued that at least two of Nancy's successors, Judy Bolton and Trixie Belden, are flesh-and-blood girls by comparison to the icy perfection of the blonde teen private eye.[19] Within the novels, Nancy's staunchest friends and admirers acknowledge her near-perfection: "Which mystery does my lady wish to solve today? Or shall we slay the wicked dragon — ?" asks George Fayne mockingly in a 1974 publication.[20] In fact, the only thing that truly upsets the "world's most famous girl detective," as Ned Nickerson labels her, is not having a case to work on. A conventional ending in the Drew books has Nancy experiencing something very close to anomie when she wraps up her investigation. Put more positively, she yearns for her next mystery. At the end of one story a histrionic actor quotes Shakespeare's *King John*:

> The day shall not be up so soon as I,
> To try the fair adventure of tomorrow.

Nancy agrees wholeheartedly; she says she *needs* a new mystery.[21]

Nancy Drew's independence is apparent in various spheres. For one, she seems to be above or beyond school. It is true that she does take summer vacations — in a contemporary book, *The Sinister Omen*, she specifically takes a spring vacation in Fort Lauderdale — but veteran readers of the series must ask, "vacation from what?" Like the Hardy Boys, Nancy has aged a bit in her fifty-plus years of investigating crime, from sixteen to eighteen. (This "growth" took place in the 1950s and may have had something to do with alterations in driving laws.) But for all intents and purposes she is free of such mundane occupations as going to school and in this way differs from the other series heroes and heroines under consideration.

She is not, however, completely free of adult "supervision," a word used loosely in this instance. She must do her detecting within the eye of the law. In the early volumes of the series, Nancy's relationship with local officials was as shaky as Frank and Joe Hardy's; the always Irish cops were of little assistance and sometimes hindered her. But in time Chief McGinnis and Nancy struck up a very good working relationship, to the point of becoming downright chummy. In *Forgotten City*, they chat away on the telephone, the chief complimenting the girl at every turn of the conversation.

Nancy's nuclear family arrangement, too, allows for maximum self-direction. She is not an orphan like Ruth Fielding and other forerunners in girls' series, but she might as well be when it comes to having free rein. Keene writes, "Left motherless at an early age [pinpointed at three in other books] Nancy had developed a fine sense of responsibility and more than earned her right to complete freedom."[22] Hannah Gruen, the Drews' housekeeper, plays the role of surrogate mother. Hannah, like Aunt Gertrude in the Hardy Boys series, spends most of her time cooking. Probably because she does not prepare meals for growing boys, Hannah Gruen's menus run less along the meat-and-potato lines — e.g., waffles, cheese soufflé, tea sandwiches, seafood quiche. She does fret about Nancy's safety, but precisely because of her subservient status — she *is* the Drews' employee — she offers no real opposition. (The Stratemeyer Syndicate came to favor a nonnuclear familial arrangement in its series; many of the young heroes and especially heroines lived with an aunt, uncle, or guardian rather than parents. Carolyn Keene's other girl detectives, the Dana Girls, reside with their Uncle Ned and his maid Cora Appel.)

Nancy, to be sure, has one parent very much on the scene. Carson Drew, distinguished lawyer, not only channels cases to his daughter, as Fenton Hardy did to his sons; he also collaborates with her on investigations, seeks her counsel regarding his own work, and always pays attention and tribute to his talented offspring. More important, he never tells her to stay out of trouble or treats her like a child. When the Drew series began, the idea of a generation gap was not a widespread notion.[23] In the Drew household, it has never materialized. Indeed, it can be asked if the two Drews don't behave more like husband and wife than father and daughter. At the conclusion of *Broken Locket* there is a cozy scene: Nancy slips into her father's study where he relaxes in his lounging robe, snuggles down in a big chair, and rests her head on his shoulder. The two look into the fire and think of broken lockets and broken hearts. And this secure arrangement is locked up. Only once that I know of did another woman try to insinuate herself into the scene. A twenty-four-year-old platinum blond lawyer named Marty King entered the picture in *Glowing Eye*, but in the end Nancy won again:

> "I'd like to speak to Marty."
> There was a pause, then Mr. Drew said, "She's no longer working here."
>   . . .
> Nancy was smiling to herself and delighted that Marty King had left her father's employ.
> "Nancy dear, I may as well tell you the whole story," her father went on. "I'm embarrassed about it, but what brought on my asking Marty to leave was" — there was a long pause — "when Marty asked me to marry her!"
>   . . .
> "Dad," she said, "if you ever want to find me a new mother, please promise me she won't be someone who tries to solve my mysteries!"
> Her father laughed heartily. "I promise," he said. (pp. 180–181)

The third area in which Nancy exercises utmost control and independence is the one that finally tripped up Ruth Fielding: relationships with the opposite sex of the same generation. By choice, she has been many times a bridesmaid but never a bride, and why should she be? Her life, as it stands, is a perfect blend of domestic harmony and thrilling mystery. Ned Nickerson, her "special friend" since the beginning of the series, would like Nancy to see matters differently. He periodically presses his case, but Nancy adroitly sidesteps his leading conversation — sometimes she even resorts to playing dumb. Somewhat surprisingly, this wonder-girl is not above girlish reaction when it comes to the subject of boys; her usual response to Ned's remarks is to flush crimson or blush to the roots of her hair. Still, Nickerson, football star at Emerson University though he may be, has never been anything but Nancy's factotum. His stock role is to play Della Street to her Perry Mason. In contemporary English mysteries for girls, the teenage investigator has not a boyfriend but a dog as a companion. Nancy, too, has a canine friend; her terrier Togo has been with her since the 1940s. And, at bottom, she has a puppy dog in Ned, who is ever faithful, obedient, affectionate, and secondary in status. In *Crumbling Wall*, he is particularly inconspicuous, interacting with Nancy only by long-distance correspondence.

Ned has gained stature in the history of the series. Carolyn Keene once wrote an essay about the series — or at least her handwritten signature is printed at the end of the essay much as Betty Crocker signs her cake-mix boxes — and in it she admits that early on "Ned was an ineffectual partner, so I made him more virile and at times he rescues Nancy just in time from a near-fatal predicament."[24] Furthermore, he is allowed to kiss Miss Drew these days. But sexual interest or emotional involvement on her part is out of the question.[25] If Nancy were truly attracted to Ned, there would be the danger of the dilemma that tortured Ruth Fielding — that is, the conflict between independence (through work or detection) and the ties of a family. Carolyn Keene's character simply avoids the issue.

The lasting effect of Nancy Drew's all-encompassing independence is that she can be supremely active and mobile, free-wheeling in a word. Always on the go, she merely stops in at home to refuel and collect late-breaking news about her cases from Carson Drew. Then she is off again in her car, or her motorboat, or her plane. Thus the automobile is the ideal icon for Nancy, and her skillful manipulation of it, a fitting indication of her independence. In *The Sign of the Twisted Candles* the heroine displays the range of her automotive know-how. First she gets into trouble while driving during a summer storm: "the wheels, sending sheets of water fender-high, skidded sickeningly." But Nancy manages to extricate herself and her passengers from danger. Then she proceeds to diagnose the roadster's difficulty—"'Oh, pshaw!' Nancy exclaimed in vexation. 'I guess the distributor got wet'"—and does the repair work herself.[26]

Interestingly, the style of Carolyn Keene's prose jibes beautifully with Nancy's active and mobile nature. Keene wastes little space in description of people or events. She devotes more attention to description of setting. Thus the energy level of her novels is high; characters move quickly through episode after episode. A side effect of this emphasis on rapid, no-frills storytelling is that readers hardly know what Nancy looks like. As in the fairy tales, where princesses are "small" or "good" or "fair" and that is all, Nancy's looks are identified only by short, repeated phrases; her face, for example, is many times described as "not beautiful but interesting." This level of description is appropriate, for a superheroine should be known not for details of appearance or manner but for bold action.

The most notable stylistic feature in Keene's writing, again, underscores Nancy's extraordinary level of activity. In an earlier chapter Keene's favorite grammatical construction, the introductory participial phrase, was labeled the "Nancy Drewster" because it is so predominant in this series. Here are a few examples from *Crumbling Wall*:

Reaching sufficient altitude, she banked and headed in the direction of Heath Castle.

Closely pursued by the barking dogs, the three girls raced madly to the front wall of the estate.

Scrambling safely over it, they paused, gasping for breath.

As the third sentence, with its additional phrase at the end, demonstrates especially well, this structure is one that allows the writer to fill her prose with active verbs. The main verb "paused" notwithstanding, the sentence leaves the girls with little time to pause, reflect, or rest.

Despite the frenetic energy of the plot and its heroine, a Nancy Drew novel quietly conveys an underlying solidity. Take Nancy's ability to judge character without fail, or the clear-cut depiction of villains as social outcasts or misfits in the River Heights milieu, or the essential security of the Drew household — all these elements bespeak a bedrock of firmly held beliefs about what is right and what is wrong, who is the right sort of person and who is not. Nancy is a Brahmin in her society. (Harriet Stratemeyer Adams once stated that were her fictional daughter to mature beyond eighteen she would go to "Wellesley, of course."[27]) Her values, and correspondingly those on which this mystery series is built, are conservative even as she seemingly projects a new approach to gender roles.

Nancy is altruistic, always eager to help others through her sleuthing, but whose cause does she champion? Down-and-out aristocrats like the proud and cultured Marches in *Old Attic*, who by birth deserve to have their missing fortunes restored, their properties reclaimed. Conversely, the evildoers in this series, from the Topham family in the first title on, are social climbers out to insinuate themselves by false scheming into higher echelons of the perfectly acceptable status quo. In the early years of the series, it has been well documented, Nancy Drew exhibited a distinct prejudice against ethnic and racial minorities — blacks, Jews, Italians, and Irish, most obviously.[28] Now the egregious bigotry has disappeared, but fundamental beliefs about social propriety remain the same. The value system inherent in the Drew books is nicely summed up by one of the most prevalent images in the series: the great house now in decay and overgrown by unruly shrubs and weeds. It is part of Nancy's role as detective to do the "landscaping" necessary to restore the fine old house to its former glory and its rightful owners, as she aims to do with Heath Castle in *Crumbling Wall*.

Thoughts of landscaping bring up the subject of setting in

the Nancy Drew books. River Heights is to Nancy as Bayport is to the Hardys, a steady and supportive home base from which to operate. Like Frank and Joe, she has traveled out from her hometown increasingly since the 1960s; in fact, she was off to New Orleans in 1945 in *The Ghost of Blackwood Hall*. But wherever she goes, River Heights is always the starting block and the finishing line for her investigations, and it provides a stable frame of reference regarding Nancy's previous accomplishments and instilled values. In this respect it functions like Alice's above-ground world in Lewis Carroll's fantasy or Dorothy's home base, Kansas, in *The Wonderful Wizard of Oz* — at the outset of the series River Heights is, by the way, placed in the Midwest, though later its location is less clear.[29] There is, however, an important distinction. Nancy has everything she wants in River Heights: security, independence, approbation, and mystery. She does not need a Wonderland or Emerald City; thus, more often than not there is no trip beyond her immediate surroundings.

Arthur Prager has gone so far as to compare River Heights with the land of Oz in terms of their common remoteness from the world readers live in: "like the land of Oz, Nancy Drew country is in another time dimension, untouched by the outside world."[30] This is not exactly so; for example, there is brief mention of the Depression, or at least its effects on certain characters' lives, in the volumes published in the 1930s, and today high tech has invaded River Heights in *Ancient Disguise*. Nonetheless, in terms of the series' spirit, Prager's comment is on the mark. River Heights has always seemed a little "out of it" in the twentieth century, a place where teas and charmingly decorated drawing rooms matter. What is more, it inevitably strikes readers as a playground, an isolated fantasy world made to order for Nancy's constant amusement. Why should she want to leave this world for Oz?[31]

As a backdrop for Nancy Drew's activities, then, River Heights is a significant aspect of Keene's formulaic mysteries. But it does not cast or create any particular atmosphere for the mysterious action. The books *do* have atmosphere. The threatening mood of the Gothic novel laces the adventure in almost every title. Adjectives like "eerie," "weird," "creepy," and "spooky" crop up everywhere in the writing, and publicists have chosen the word "spinetingling" to describe the series in their blurbs on the back covers of the books. Spinetingling? — well, not entirely. Nancy's matter-of-fact reaction to skeletons, glowing eyes, and potential ghosts becalms the anxious, horrific atmosphere on many occasions. Still, the Gothic trappings favored by Keene, especially when coupled with magical clues, fresh footprints, and other accoutrements of the mystery genre, do contribute to the suspense. Together, the formulaic ingredients of Gothic and detective fiction leave Nancy perpetually caught up in a cycle of chasing (or being chased), confinement in scary circumstances, and escape by means of strenuous struggle. This seesaw pattern of pursuit, confinement, and release, in turn, wrings out readers' emotions by exciting alternating feelings of tension and exhilaration.[32]

Exactly what are the Gothic elements in the Nancy Drew series? Foremost, there are innumerable antiquated inns and manor houses whose true ownership and other secrets Nancy investigates, places with such names as Twisted Candles Inn, Pine Hill, Lilac Inn, Pleasant Hedges, Moonstone Castle, and — in *Crumbling Wall* — Heath Castle. Nancy once in a while goes treasure- or secret-hunting in a cave (the one at Bald Head Cliff in *Tolling Bell*, for example) or an underground reservoir (see *The Mysterious Mannequin*), but she does not rival the Hardy Boys in this regard. Her preferred place of confinement, where she spends a substantial period of time in most of her mysteries, is the cobwebbed attic, the dank cellar, the castle tower, the secret chamber, the hidden staircase, the locked closet — in sum, the stock haunts of the Gothic novel. And like the motherless heroines of the Gothics, Nancy normally enters old houses *alone* in search of clues to the activities or motives of (usually male) figures.

Other Gothic conditions prevail in the Drew books. Ominous voices murmur "N-a-a-ancy" or warn her away from her search, ghostly footsteps are heard in other rooms. Once the young detective is pursued by a driverless red car; another time she is chased by a puppet across a moonlit lawn. There have been hexes in Pennsylvania Dutch country and séances in New Orleans. Clammy hands and bony fingers regularly brush against her face and fumble for her throat. Finally, the weather around

River Heights seems especially stormy, mainly after dark.

Stories of domestic detection have a long history among female writers and readers; and this is not surprising given the fact that household settings were the norm in nineteenth-century women's fiction. It was only a small departure to introduce the mysterious crime into the daily routine of these "interior" tales, as did Mrs. Henry Wood in *East Lynne* or Mary Elizabeth Braddon in *Lady Audley's Secret*. Nor was Carolyn Keene the originator of the hybrid Gothic mystery. American predecessor Mary Roberts Rinehart had begun to combine sensational Gothic ingredients with mystery plots nearly a quarter of a century before Nancy Drew solved *The Secret of the Old Clock*. Rinehart's titles alone suggest similarities between her mysteries of family secrets and many of the Nancy Drew books: *The Circular Staircase, The Album, The Red Lamp, Episode of the Wandering Knife, The Window at the White Cat*.[33] To explore but one of these, *The Red Lamp* contains the now empty home of a gentleman (Twin Hollows) that itself holds a dim figure standing at the foot of its staircase; then there is the semimagical object referred to in the title, which so resembles one of Nancy Drew's clues. Keene's second book, *The Hidden Staircase*, written in 1930 just five years after Rinehart's, makes use of similar Gothic iconography, right down to the name of the decaying estate. Hers is called Twin Oaks.

The appearance of an adolescent heroine in a Gothic tale is something else that is not unique to the Nancy Drew series. The first Gothic, Radcliffe's late eighteenth-century *The Mysteries of Udolpho*, is the story of a young heroine named Emily St. Aubert and her suitor Chevalier Valancourt. The adolescent girl is a natural character in stories that are fairly transparent explorations of the mysteries of sexual awakening and its attendant psychological fears. Tales of confinement in gloomy castles owned by dark but gentlemanly strangers are certainly related to the fairy tale Beauty and the Beast, the classic eighteenth-century text of which first appeared in a girls' magazine.[34] That story, too, concerns the psychology of first love — the young Beauty is both attracted to and repulsed by her Beast.[35]

These are Nancy Drew's antecedents, but it cannot be forgotten that the Stratemeyer series is Gothicized detection from which all prospect of growing up and sexual discovery has been removed and that psychological distress will never be known by the outgoing, no-nonsense girl detective. A Nancy Drew novel is to the truly terrifying Gothic tale as Walt Disney's whitewashed visualization of the fairy-tale Snow White is to the earlier and violent story of jealousy and maturation collected by the Grimms. Nancy has transcended terror as surely as she has overcome the need for money, for boys, for anything she does not already have. Living in the nearly fantastic land of River Heights, she is hermetically sealed off from change, growth, failure. And her chosen avocation — private, nonprofit investigation — is a curiously unrealistic endeavor itself. Very few girls, or boys either for that matter, really grow up to become detectives. As a symbolic figure, however, the young female private eye is everything girl readers could ask for, combining "all the energy and purposefulness of the working girl and none of her restrictions."[36]

Nancy Drew, in summary, is a fantasy figure who is a worthy successor to the Stratemeyer Syndicate's first female superstar, Ruth Fielding. But Ruth, like so many of the career girl detectives in series books popular during and after World War II, finally got caught in the middle of real-life dilemmas: she was divided between, on the one hand, being an independent career woman (and sometimes sleuth) and, on the other, moving along the course traditionally taken by women to marriage and children. The tomboy or the lady? — as other girls' books of the 1920s and 1930s framed the question. For Nancy Drew, there is no such dilemma, though the opposition is represented in her series by the detective's two friends, boyish George Fayne and plump and giggly Bess Marvin.

As do much popular film and fiction, the Nancy Drew novels offer an escapist fantasy, and they allay their readers' real ambitions and doubts with a vision of a mythic heroine who is immensely talented and virtually omnipotent. There is, ultimately, an interesting irony underlying Nancy Drew and the success of her series. It would seem that the transition from the heroines of nineteenth-century domestic fiction — so limited in their choices — to the supremely confident and independent girl investigator represents an expansion of possibilities regarding both literary characterization and its effects on readers. Nancy is not socially confined to houses or domestic situations as were the females in sentimental fiction that prevailed, in girls' books anyway, on into the twentieth century, as demonstrated by Pollyanna or Rebecca of Sunnybrook Farm. Nor is she trapped physically or psychologically within quarters. This was the fate of the orphaned heroines who moved into rich men's houses in the Gothic novels that replaced sentimental fiction and have remained popular with young and mature female readers throughout Nancy Drew's reign — for example, Daphne du Maurier's *Rebecca*, written in 1938 and turned into a superbly terrifying Gothic film by Alfred Hitchcock two years later. Unlike the normally blonde stars of Hitchcock's thrillers Nancy can find her way out of scary houses and haunted inns/motels.[37] And as for being trapped in an oppressive life, that is simply the antithesis of Nancy's charmed existence. Yet . . . it is precisely because she is so far removed from the little qualms and the big frustrations and decisions facing real girls and women that she cannot be considered a helpful fictional model of successful womanhood, the fact that she has been praised in the pages of *Ms.* notwithstanding.[38]

Like Carroll's *Alice* books, the Nancy Drew novels depict a resourceful and imaginative heroine in action in a place where special rules operate — namely River Heights, where crooks always give in to determined girls. But neither Carolyn Keene nor Lewis Carroll takes issue with the social, moral, and gender values dominant at the time she or he wrote. Alice and her readers must return to Victorian England and become proper ladies. Nancy gets to stay in her playground indefinitely, but readers must move on. To what? If we extrapolate from the cultural assumptions behind Keene's series, Nancy Drew would, as Mason first observed,[39] grow up to be like Mrs. Bobbsey in another Stratemeyer series — pretty, demure, completely forgettable. She is saved from that fate, but there is nothing in her series to make us believe that its creators would have things any other way for the vast young female readership that devours the books.

Of course, only tiresome adult rereaders of Nancy Drew will raise such questions, the same kind of critic who would pity the Hardy Boys' fate of being confined to endless reruns of their adventures. Girls hooked on the series will continue to revel in traveling to River Heights, where life is at once safely predictable and excitingly mysterious and where criminal activity is both intriguing and easily dealt with. For preteens, unsure of their footing in their own surroundings, Nancy's ability to triumph over wicked, grown men and emerge from dangerous encounters unscathed is as reassuring and confidence-inspiring as it is thrilling. These encounters, and their easy outcomes, may not mirror those that will face readers, but the teen detective's quick thinking and fancy footwork go beyond providing an afternoon's fun. They do suggest, in bold and fantastic relief, patterns of active exploration of the world and the questions it presents.

As for the matter of getting "hooked" on the series, readers don't stay under the spell for long. Children's librarians tell me that Nancy's appeal evaporates somewhere around the fifth year of elementary schooling. Then the girls who fantasized with Nancy Drew will seek literary pleasure and encouragement elsewhere — in the adolescent novel, in adult popular fiction, in historical fiction and biography, in the classics, in true fantasy literature. Author Frances Fitzgerald confesses to shucking her Nancy Drews around age twelve for the Gothic governess and her demon lover.[40] But as she goes on to say, "we can't really have forgotten Nancy Drew or abandoned her completely for Jane [Eyre]. . . . They complement each other. One is an Enlightenment child — rational, secure, active. The other, a Romantic — sensuous, vulnerable, ruled by passion." Whatever literary or life experiences readers graduate to, Nancy does seem to be in American girls' bloodstream; and as part of their larger reading and developmental pattern, she not only has won — but *has* — her place.

The Happy Hollisters (original book jacket).

—*The Happy Hollisters*
Jerry West
Garden City Book, 1953

7

THE HAPPY HOLLISTERS
Mystery for the Entire Family

"Blackmar?" Ricky asked. "Who is he?"
Meyer smiled, heaved a long sigh, and sat back in his chair. "Maybe I
shouldn't bore you," he said, "because it has to do with detective work."
"Detectives!" Holly blurted. "We're detectives, Mr. Meyer."
"Honest we are," Pete said. "We love to solve mysteries."

— The Happy Hollisters and
the Swiss Echo Mystery

The Stratemeyer Syndicate did not confine itself to teenage sleuths. Mysteries had a proven track record with readers of the series discussed in earlier chapters—why not with their younger brothers and sisters? And so in 1935, the Syndicate offered a new series, The Mary and Jerry Mystery Stories, starring the young twins of the Denton family. In Francis Hunt's series, which contains only five volumes, the protagonists do their sleuthing "between school hours," and the detection seems decidedly low-keyed when compared with the criminal activity encountered by the Hardys, Nancy Drew, Ruth Fielding, or the Rovers. Mary and Jerry search for a missing clown, a parrot stolen from a pet shop, a purloined piggy bank. Further evidence that Stratemeyer felt there was a market for mysteries among elementary schoolers can be found in the histories of already popular series for that age group.

At about the time the Hardy Boys and Nancy Drew first began their investigations, Laura Lee Hope's long-standing and highly successful Bobbsey Twins books took on some of the traits of the mystery genre.[1] Titles written in the first two decades of the century routinely depicted the two sets of Bobbsey Twins — Nan and Bert and Freddie and Flossie — enjoying fairly aimless vacation adventures . . . at the county fair, at Meadow Brook Farm, on Blueberry Island, etc. But by 1934 true tales of detection appear — e.g., *The Bobbsey Twins Solve a Mystery*, *The Bobbsey Twins at Mystery Mansion*.[2] Since that time — i.e., for fifty years now — the Bobbsey Twins have remained detectives. In the 1980s they have been busy tracking down a missing blue poodle, art thieves in Bermuda, and a stolen dune buggy, among other things. Likewise, in the 1950s the Stratemeyer Syndicate recycled one of its very popular heroines, Helen Louise Thorndyke's Honey Bunch. She was reborn as a sleuth in the Honey Bunch and Norman series, in which Honey Bunch Morton and her playmate Norman Clark "play detective at Niagara Falls" and solve mysteries surrounding pine cones, walnut trees, and paper lanterns.[3] It was in 1953, however, that the Syndicate issued volume 1 of the Happy Hollisters line, which became the first best seller featuring, from the outset, young children in mystery adventures.

The Happy Hollisters, written by Syndicate partner Andrew Svenson under the pen name Jerry West, would continue for seventeen years and thirty-three volumes. Thus the series stands as one of the few recent supersuccesses created by the house of Stratemeyer, which after World War II has thrived, by and large, on the continuous popularity of series that began before the Depression. In a letter written in 1969 toward the end of the Happy Hollisters' productive period, Svenson notes that more than a million copies of Hollisters books were then being sold annually by Doubleday through their book club. He goes on to make grand claims for his series: "this series is undoubtedly the most popular in the United States for younger children, and educators tell me it has a tremendous impact on the youth of today."[4] Maybe so, for fourteen years after the last volume, *The Happy Hollisters and the Mystery of the Midnight Trolls*, was published, the series still actively circulates at many public libraries. But when the Happy Hollisters are read and reread after the eminently more thrilling Hardy Boys and Drew books, they seem by comparison tame in their trotting out of the same formulas of plotting and characterization, this time in the most reduced variations.

It is this boiled-down quality of the Happy Hollisters series that makes it deserving of critical consideration. Beyond their one-time boom and ongoing popularity, these books demonstrate, within, why the mystery genre appeals to beginning readers; in fact, they suggest the most basic attraction any kind of reading has for the eager and uninitiated beginner. The Hollisters volumes are about searches and investigations, and the word that best sums up the five Hollister siblings is "curious." The patterns of discovery that prevail in the books are, writ large, those underlying most children's literature — something puzzling is figured out, a problematic circumstance or event is put in perspective, a wrong is righted. The act of reading itself is a process of detecting or exploring, and ultimately mastering, the previously hidden. The Happy Hollisters series offers puzzles that are zero-grade as regards their degree of difficulty and a domestic setting so cozy that it cushions the task of discovery facing protagonists and readers by placing it in a context of security and encouragement.

The Happy Hollisters at Sea Gull Beach, the third volume in the series, was written in 1953 and is still in print.[5] The novel opens with a characteristic street scene in front of the Hollisters' home in Shoreham. The two oldest children, Pete (age twelve) and Pam (age ten) are roller skating when the promise of adventure comes their way, in the form of a letter from their Uncle Russ postmarked at Sea Gull Beach. Russ Hollister fits every child's dream of a perfect uncle: he is a young, good-looking, and energetic cartoonist for a nearby newspaper, who can be counted on to supply excitement and mystery for his nieces and nephews. His letter, which is printed verbatim in the story, reads:

> Last week I came upon a group here who are looking for a pirate ship named the *Mystery*. It was wrecked one hundred years ago, and they're sure it must be buried somewhere in this area. How would you like to visit me for a short vacation and hunt for the treasure ship, too? Ask mother and dad to bring you.
>
> With love,
> Uncle Russ (pp. 6–7)

The five Hollisters—Pete, Pam, Ricky (age seven), Holly (age six), and Sue (age four)— beg their father to go. Hard-working John Hollister, who is busy at his combination hardware, toy, and sporting goods store, The Trading Post, says maybe. Meanwhile the young Hollisters decide to stage a pirate play as a kind of dry run for their Sea Gull Beach expedition. Never ones to do things halfway, they turn their rehearsals into a public performance, complete with props and costumes, put on for the benefit of the Crippled Children's Hospital. They even manage to gain a creditable performance from the neighborhood bully, Joey Brill, their antagonist throughout the series.

In chapter 3 a package arrives for the children's mother, Elaine Hollister. It is a ceramic lamp shaped like a lighthouse that has been sent by benevolent Uncle Russ. When the family collie Zip knocks the lamp over, Pete attempts to mend it—and finds something green protruding from the clay. "'Say,' he cried, 'it looks like an emerald!'" (p. 42) A local jeweler confirms Pete's intuition. Now there's no stopping the Hollister children from conducting a search at Sea Gull Beach. Mr. Hollister has little choice, he has been outnumbered.

En route, the Hollisters, and the treasure hunt, stop a while at a pony corral. Sue's mount takes off, but she is rescued by the quick rope work of her brother Ricky. Then the family stops again, this time at the guest house of generous Mrs. Worth, who makes dinner for them, and room where there is none. Finally, they come upon a sign reading

WELCOME TO SEA GULL BEACH

The Hollister children befriend Rachel Snow at the beach, and Holly explains their mission to her bluntly: "We've come to visit our uncle and find the pirate treasure" (p. 59). Rachel tells them that people have been diving for the treasure for a long time, but to no avail. In fact, they are at that moment being spied upon by Homer Ruffly, the son of the head of one such treasure-hunting party. Beyond providing necessary background information, Rachel also happens to be the granddaughter of the woman who made the lighthouse lamp. But before she takes them to her grandmother, there is another time-out from sleuthing. The children play at the beach and come up with the shell of a horseshoe crab, a starfish, a live crab, and a jarful of periwinkles.

Even at play, the Hollisters have a knack for striking it rich.

Soon they pay Rachel's relative a visit. Grandma Alden tells them that she thinks the emerald is part of the pirate treasure from the lost *Mystery*; every once in a while a gem is found on the local beach, it turns out. This is all the incentive the Hollisters need to renew their search. First they seek a character named Scowbanger, who supplies Mrs. Alden's clay. He entertains the children by showing them how his beach buggy runs and then obligingly takes them to the shore area where he dug his clay. Within minutes, Holly unearths the lid of a brass box. Once again, however, the search party is being spied upon. What is more, Holly disappears shortly after making her discovery. As it happens, she has merely wandered off into the forest hunting for the perfect pine cone — abduction is out of the question in this series.

Narrative action resumes, now offshore. Uncle Russ wants to sketch a deep-sea diver and so asks Scowbanger to outfit himself as one. The old salt agrees, but when he actually goes down under, his air system is sabotaged, somewhat unwittingly, by Homer Ruffly. Next, the boys fly kites and the girls build sand castles. Then the boys go aquaplaning, while Rachel and Pam continue inspection of local sand dunes. Pam topples from the summit of one, grabs at a stick as she falls, and exclaims, "This is part of an old oar. And it has letters on it — MYS. Do you suppose it could be from the pirate ship *Mystery*?" (p. 119) Chapter 11 ends on this suspenseful note. Rachel answers her friend's question at the outset of the next chapter, "It's a wonderful clue! . . . Maybe the old pirate ship is buried right here!"

Fortified by a sea clam pie Grandma Alden has baked for them, the brood continues their exploration. Homer's father has been impressed by the young search team's efforts thus far and offers to join forces with them. Nothing doing, say the Hollisters, and so the race and its contestants are clearly lined up. Even Zip gets into a fight with the Rufflys' Airedale.

Uncle Russ's wife Marge and two children join the others at Sea Gull Beach, and thus two new detectives, Jean and Teddy, are taken on. They all troop out to a farmer's field to explore a house on the property. Grandma Alden had said that one survivor of the *Mystery* had been found by a couple living in a house that fits the description of this one. In the cellar, the children immediately find a marble slab affording a major clue. "Read what it says," begs Holly, and readers get the chance to do just that for, again, the clue is literally spelled out:

> A Mystery Man
> Though a Pirate he be
> Loved his Ship and the Stormy Sea
> All was lost on the Bounding Main
> Where the Frog Rock looks Across to Spain. (p. 151)

All that stands between the Hollister family and treasure is a rock in the shape of a frog. A final pause in the search comes at this climactic point, and the seven children are alternately treated to a helicopter ride that allows them to spy on a black whale, which spews accommodatingly at them. The next day Zip finds the Frog Rock. After further mischief from Homer Ruffly (and a hurricane thrown in for suspense), the team of detectives tend to their final digging near Frog Rock:

> "Where'll we start digging?" Ricky asked.
> "Let's start at this low spot," Pete said, pointing out a large area where the wind had already helped to dig a big hole some distance back from the water.
> Their shovels began to fly and the hole in the sand grew deeper. Suddenly Ricky's spade hit something. He picked it up. Two old coins!
> "Look what I've found!" he shouted.
> The others ran to his side and Pete examined the dull brown-colored coins.
> "They have Spanish words on them!" he said excitedly. "We must be near the pirate treasure!" (p. 176)

They are, and soon they have come upon the wreckage of the ship itself, including the boat's prow with *Mystery* in big copper letters. Mr. Ruffly intrudes at this point, but the Mayor of Sea Gull Beach corroborates the Hollisters' claim. Then a broken mast is uncovered, and a small box full of jewels. In the end the town council decides to leave the treasure ship where the Hollisters found it and turn it into a park. And the community offers three cheers for the young detectives.

A quick search through the thirty-three titles in the Happy Hollisters series reveals a striking resemblance between the contents of these novels and the Hardy Boys books. The quest for missing treasure in one form or another provides the dominant plot line. Hence it is appropriate that the dust jacket of the first volume shows the children in the midst of a game of hide-and-seek; that game is the prototype for all their later play at being detectives. The series includes a number of seaside (or, at least, sea-oriented) treasure hunts. After *Sea Gull Beach* came *The Happy Hollisters at Circus Island*, *The Happy Hollisters and the Old Clipper Ship*, *The Happy Hollisters at Lizard Cove*, *The Happy Hollisters and the Mystery of the Little Mermaid*, and *The Happy Hollisters and the Sea Turtle Mystery*. But most of the other volumes turn out to be treasure tales as well; for example, the initial mystery, *The Happy Hollisters*, concerns uncanny events at the family's new Shoreham home, events connected with valuables hidden there. Over the years the Hollister children, moreover, prove themselves prodigies when it comes to archaeology — they like nothing better than digging, which is, after all, a literal manifestation of what being a detective is about. Sometimes their digging leads to a little historical detective work. In *The Happy Hollisters and the Secret Fort* the five children singlehandedly uncover Fort Freedom, a pre-Revolutionary War settlement that had theretofore eluded all discovery efforts. In the process they learn about the history of their hometown Shoreham. In one of the last books in the series, *The Happy Hollisters and the Mexican Idol Mystery*, the Hollisters are involved in an investigation whose scale rivals the plot of *Raiders of the Lost Ark*; they go to Yucatan and there lead adults to a previously unexplored Maya temple, at the same time foiling the efforts of crooks to find the place first and loot it.

The children find secrets begging to be brought to light close to Shoreham, but they more often encounter puzzles while off on family vacations, or when the family accompanies Mr. Hollister on a business trip. When they go to Europe with their father to look for merchandise to sell at The Trading Post, they walk into a mystery concerning cuckoo clocks in the Black Forest and then turn around and get involved with an international diamond thief in Switzerland.[6] Analogously, they seem to be able to sniff out missing goods at any time of the year. There is a strong seasonal emphasis in this series, stemming from the books' membership in the ranks of family fiction. In this literature the shifting patterns of domestic activity throughout the year contribute if not a plot, at least a basic rhythm to the narrative. In the Happy Hollisters this seasonal procession is stretched out — in fact, it repeats itself several times — over the length of the series. The majority of titles, *Sea Gull Beach* among them, depict the family on summer vacation; others are built around winter events (e.g., *The Happy Hollisters at Snowflake Camp*, *The Happy Hollisters and the Ice Carnival Mystery*). Specific holidays can also shape the mystery at hand. In *The Happy Hollisters and the Trading Post Mystery* a Santa Claus display that sat atop their father's store is stolen; in *The Happy Hollisters and the Mystery of the Golden Witch* a bejeweled weather vane in the shape of a witch is the treasure the children discover at Halloween.

The mystery plots — that is, the treasure hunts — that supply the backbone for series stories are always tempered by a sizeable number of what might be called family-fun scenes. Daily life for the Hollister children, who never fight or even bicker, is reminiscent of an ongoing birthday party attended by well-adjusted, carefree, and gregarious youngsters. They prepare skits, have fun with their pets, play with their many toys, and have popcorn and pink lemonade before going to bed. Reading one of Jerry West's novels, one encounters continual breaks in the linear searches for treasure, breaks that simply describe the children at play. These narrative pauses help to defer the solution of a not very complicated mystery, but they are important for another reason, too: they set the secure frame in which all investigations of the mysterious are conducted. Toys and pets are important parts of young children's world. The Hollisters, whose good fortune it is to have a father in the business of toys, are well-supplied in that department. They have a host of animals to play with as well. Initially, there was Zip the collie. Then the family moved to Shoreham (in the first volume of the series), where they acquired White Nose and her five kittens. Later came Domingo the burro, who lives in a stall in the garage. Furthermore, individual books introduce pets in cameo roles — e.g., Lucky the Lizard in *Lizard Cove*, a family of ground hogs in *The Happy Hollisters and the Whistle-Pig Mystery*. Both their toys and their pets are familiar accessories in the moments of family fun that punctuate the mystery plot.

Accordingly, there are few subplots in a Happy Hollisters mystery. Where Stratemeyer mystery series for older readers depend on presentation of assorted unusual happenings and characters that are gradually shown to be interconnected, the Hollisters' investigations are one-track. In *Sea Gull Beach*, the missing pirate ship is the only issue in question. Extraordinary events transpire — an emerald pops up in a lamp, a boy spies on their sleuthing, a marble marker with a mysterious inscription is found — but all of these are directly, and clearly, related to unearthing the wrecked ship and the riches it holds. No contrapuntal or confusing rhythms here, just the straightforward melody. The mystery is so simple, in fact, that a dog can — and does — solve it.

An interesting aspect of the formulaic clues in this series is their visual quality. Clues in all Stratemeyer mysteries tend to be tangible objects that substitute for any sort of subtle slips in conversation or behavior that might tip off a detective inclined toward nice deduction or delicate psychological inference. West's series takes the process of objectifying clues one step further. He literally presents them in boldface type, as demonstrated by the inscription on the marble marker in *Sea Gull Beach*. When Sue Hollister trips in a graveyard in *Golden Witch*, she falls onto a stone that says:

Adam Cornwall
Who Reads My Stone and Drops a Tear
May Find a Treasure in the Air.[7]

In *The Happy Hollisters* there is even visual confirmation of the fact that a prowler has indeed been entering the family's house; Pete rigs up a camera that takes a perfect picture of the man — and the photograph is depicted in one of Helen S. Hamilton's illustrations.[8]

Such overt signaling of the plot's pieces helps to make the Happy Hollisters books the most unadorned variants of the mystery formula. There are no "extras" in the way of subplots, and what is there is presented with bold announcement of key ingredients. In *Sea Gull Beach* the young detectives are out to discover a boat named *Mystery*. How much plainer can the scheme be? In addition to highlighting the mystery elements in the novel, West sees to it that other turns in the narrative are marked — for example, that sign that is both pictured and written out in the text when the Hollisters arrive at a new setting: WELCOME TO SEA GULL BEACH. In all these ways the book is made, in modern parlance, "user-friendly." The story can be managed by the youngest, most inexperienced reader. And at the end of the search in any Happy Hollisters title what has happened is rehearsed at disproportionate length just to assure that the reader leaves the book with full mastery of the mystery and a sense of unity or order as great as that existing within the Hollister household. In *The Happy Hollisters and the Mystery in Skyscraper City*, for instance, the "thoroughly dejected and frightened" culprit says, "I want to get it off my chest. I'll tell you everything."[9] That in itself is not surprising for a Stratemeyer publication, but what follows is unusual: a three-page question and answer session in which he comes close to explaining exactly how the plot was put together.

What has already been said about Hollisters mystery plots — their unilateral nature, the many pauses for family fun, the care with which significant elements are presented — suggests something about the pace of the investigative action. It is quite slow. If reading a Rover Boys book can be compared to riding a roller coaster, reading a Happy Hollisters is like a trip on a merry-go-round — a slow and easily mapped course with only the gentlest ups and downs. (Incidentally, the tenth title in the series is *The Happy Hollisters and the Merry-Go-Round Mystery*.) Danger of any account, what is more, is conspicuously absent in these books. The children fall off sand dunes, are carried off on wild pony rides, and get lost in the woods; but unlike older series heroes and heroines, they are never physically assaulted by their adversaries or caught in any truly dire circumstances. Almost the only violence comes when Pete, at a rate of about once per book, slugs neighborhood bully Joey Brill, and that action is shown to be the retribution the boy deserves for the mischief he has made.

The regimented writing in the series complements the modulated structure and content of the books. Compared to the syntactic convolutions practiced by Arthur M. Winfield in the Rover Boys series, the prose of Jerry West is—like his plots—pared down to essentials. Beginning readers are thrown for no stylistic loops by the simple sentence patterns he favors. Even the characters utter the very same exclamations throughout the series. In every book Pete says "Crickets!" at least once; Ricky, "Yikes!" The girls are not given to such verbal flamboyance: only the baby, four-year-old Sue, talks to formula—she drops her prefixes ("How 'citing!" or "Let's have more 'ventures!") in a fashion reminiscent of Annie Fellows Johnston's Little Colonel. And Arthur Svenson scrupulously measured out his writing in this series. Notations in his typescripts indicate that he thought in terms of chapters that conformed to preestablished length.[10] The virtually identical number of pages in each book suggests that this count, too, was calculated to give readers just what they expected—namely, 184 pages, plus or minus one.

Mystery novels are notoriously dependent on coincidence. Train schedules permit criminals to make split-second getaways, circumstances conspire to make innocent people appear guilty, in the end the detective often trips up the guilty party thanks to some unforeseen occurrence beyond the clever criminal's control. In the Happy Hollisters books fortuitous coincidence—and, more broadly, good luck—runs rampant. Edward Stratemeyer had been dead thirty-three years when the first Hollisters mystery was issued, but the spirit of Horatio Alger so much in his blood is carried on in this series. Pluck and luck lead to success, specifically to the discovery of riches. This is only natural in a series about characters whose cheerfulness and optimism cast a sun-drenched aura on all proceedings. The tone of the books, to use a word Alger often chose to describe his own characters, is sanguine. Each Stratemeyer series was bound in a distinctive color, and the Hollisters books are in red, but yellow might have been the better choice, as an indicator of the unrelentingly sunny disposition of the series' characters.

The Hollisters' luck in drawing adventure their way is demonstrated at the beginning of each mystery. They have only to stand outside their house, and the invitation to seek treasure or solve a puzzle comes their direction. In *Sea Gull Beach* the mailman brings Uncle Russ's letter; in *Secret Fort* a power shovel comes down their street, and soon all five Hollisters are sitting in the cab with its operator, heading toward the site where they will eventually find the buried Fort Freedom. In *Whistle-Pig Mystery* the children see a television news story about a train robbery in New England, and the same day they receive a letter from a German woodcarver who needs the dimensions of a certain wooden Indian that turns out to be housed in a museum in Foxboro, the same place the train robbery took place. In no time they are off to Foxboro.[11] Even the villains in the series bring the Hollisters luck. In *The Happy Hollisters and the Secret of the Lucky Coins*, Joey Brill breaks the glass of a framed map that has been lent to them, a happy catastrophe since it leads to the discovery of an important deed buried behind the map.

In *Lucky Coins* the Hollisters end up finding a boxful of rare old coins that have been stolen from a local museum. The family of detectives is, in fact, extremely prone to happening upon boxes filled with precious goods. In *Lizard Cove* they find one that appears to be empty:

> "There's nothing here," Carlos said in disappointment. He looked as if he might cry.
> "Let me see it," Pete requested and Carlos stepped aside.
> After examining the inside of the box, Pete said, "Let me have your knife, Carlos. I believe the box has a false bottom."
> Hopefully Carlos handed over the knife and Pete slid it down the sides to loosen the bottom. In a few minutes the metal piece came free and the boy lifted it out.
> *Below lay a small golden crown beautifully studded with emeralds!*[12]

Horatio Alger's bootblacks and shoeshine boys were never so lucky. Of course, the Hollister children do not keep the treasure they find. (Occasionally they take a reward, a Flying Eagle cent worth four hundred dollars in *Lucky Coins*, for example. This gift leads Pete to remark, "Crickets! . . . We're rich!") Nor do they get paid for their work. They solve mysteries, instead, for the sheer fun of it, though frequently their discoveries do have the altruistic side effect of benefiting the community. This group of children has been the toast of more local officials than any of their older counterparts. Indeed, an often-used formulaic conclusion in the series is the civic celebration, at which the Hollisters are the guests of honor as in *Sea Gull Beach*.

Despite the accolades they receive and the rather surprising finds they make, Pete, Pam, Ricky, Holly, and Sue Hollister are just plain kids, and they are differentiated to an extent. The two oldest children are blonds. Pete is the protector of his younger siblings and the prime mover in most of their investigations. Pam is good-hearted and maternal, the equivalent of Nan Bobbsey in that earlier series. She looks after her younger brother and sisters and loves animals, especially the collie Zip. Ricky and Holly form the second boy-girl pairing. (Interestingly, the Syndicate has here given up its penchant for having twins appear in family-oriented series.) They are both active and sometimes mischievous. The information printed on the back of the series' dust jackets describes Ricky, the freckled and redheaded Hollister, as a "tease" and pig-tailed Holly as a "tomboy." Holly, like her older sister, spends much of her time with pets, especially her cat White Nose, whose kittens are the delight of the youngest Hollister, Sue. It can be readily observed that there is a clear-cut gender gap at work in the Happy Hollisters books, a distinction that overrides the age differences among the five children. As regards activities allotted to the siblings, for example, Pete and Ricky go off aquaplaning in *Sea Gull Beach* while the girls stay on land and quietly build sand castles. In *The Happy Hollisters and the Scarecrow Mystery* the boys go out with their father to test a new canoe in white water; the girls stay back in camp and learn how to make "beans in a hole." Some consolation!

Given the number of protagonists in the Hollister books, readers might not expect to find the support system customary in a Stratemeyer series. Nonetheless, there is a neighborhood full of playmates who appear throughout the thirty-three titles: Dave Mead, Ann and Jeff Hunter, and, of course, Joey Brill. Then there are Uncle Russ's children, Teddy and Jean Hollister. When the Hollisters go off on vacations, they always encounter other friends, like Rachel Snow in *Sea Gull Beach*. Finally, adults figure prominently in the Hollisters' mysteries. Officer Cal Newberry, a young and handsome police officer in Shoreham, is simply an overgrown playmate, and the employees at The Trading Post fit the same category. Indy Roades thinks it sounds like fun to give over his vacation to transporting the five Hollister children to New England in *Whistle-Pig Mystery*. Uncle Russ is equally willing and, further, often provides the impetus for taking off on a detecting vacation.

The children's pretty blonde mother is "always ready to meet any sudden need — for a surprise picnic or a helping hand," according to the dust jackets. Because of her good nature and immediate acquiescence to whatever the children may propose, there is no reason for her to be removed from the scene, the fate of mothers in so much children's literature. The young Hollisters have almost complete freedom to prowl as they choose; in *Lucky Coins*, for example, Mrs. Hollister agrees that they should go comb the bottom of the town fountain in the middle of the night.[13] She is the kind of mother, furthermore, who leaves directions in the kitchen so the children can make pancakes when they get up, who is available and able to chauffeur the children down Manhattan to Chinatown. (Maybe this is how Nancy Drew would have turned out, had she grown up.) Mr. Hollister is the great provider and the leader of expeditions. He is not only fun to have around, he is useful. Over and above his invention of new toys and the felicitous business trips he must make — on which he takes his family as a rule — he is the sort of man who can explain the living arrangements of raccoons:

> Mr. Hollister explained that raccoons' dens are usually in hollow trees, but sometimes they live in small caves. In either case, he said, the den would not be far from the water. "That's because most of the raccoon's food consists of frogs, turtles, mussels, or fish."
>
> "And doesn't a raccoon wash all his food before he eats it?" Mrs. Hollister asked.
>
> "That's the common belief," her husband replied, "but some woodsmen say the raccoon's food is wet because he gets it from the water, not because he's especially dainty."[14]

The Hollister family, then, is big, happy, and united. The children get along beautifully with each other and with their parents, and group solidarity supersedes individual identity. This latter point is underscored time and again, whenever they meet somebody new, in fact. Their reputation as "The Happy Hollisters" precedes them, as Scowbanger's remark in *Sea Gull Beach* illustrates:

> "Yo ho ho and a band of pirates! I'll bet these are the Happy Hollisters."
>
> Sue's eyes grew wide as saucers. "How do you know, Mr. Scowbanger?"
>
> "Good news travels fast," he replied. (p. 73)

Freud has talked about the "family romance" dreamed up by the imaginative young child, whereby he replaces, in his mind, his actual parents with ones he thinks he would prefer.[15] According to Freud, the child hypothesizes parents of a higher social status than that of his actual mother and father. The Hollisters are firmly rooted in the middle class — not the *upper* middle class of Nancy and Carson Drew — but they represent a kind of dream family for many readers of the series, who project themselves as members of this big, active, and harmonious group. In the characters' lives there are both domestic fun and big adventure in the world beyond — and there are no arguments, chores, dull and rainy afternoons, or homework to spoil the fun.[16]

The pleasures of "home sweet home" are commonplace in literature for young children. "Dulce Domum" is the motto in Kenneth Grahame's masterful presentation of the domestic life, *The Wind in the Willows*; Dorothy's words that conclude *The Wonderful Wizard of Oz* are, "And oh, Aunt Em! I'm so glad to be at home again!"[17] Inevitably in such literature, the values of the home are unobtrusively conveyed. The underlying beliefs and opinions in the Hollisters' universe are updated manifestations of what Bobbie Ann Mason has neatly termed "Bobbsey Bourgeois."[18] The Hollisters exemplify the zeitgeist of 1950s America. They go to church, are civic-minded, consume for pleasure, and — above all — do things as a family. Indeed, their unified front always makes quick work of the drifters and social outsiders who throw up obstacles in their path. The Slick Dicks, Stiltses, and Keys Cravens of Jerry West's series are essentially straw men, loners who have no chance against the combined forces of a family like the Hollisters that is, moreover, so firmly entrenched in and backed by the community. And the Hollisters are especially industrious; even their play takes the form of trial runs in free enterprise. They apply great energy to tracking down treasure, to thinking up schemes to improve business at their father's already successful store, and to planning skits for profit. In *The Happy Hollisters on a River Trip*, Ricky suggests, "Maybe we could even start a business and sell lollipops."[19]

Because of the presence of five protagonists in the Happy Hollisters mysteries, a reader can plug into the adventures at any of a number of places. The children in the stories range from four to twelve in age, and readers are likewise targeted at the first-through-fifth-grade levels. Thus there is considerable leeway for finding a suitable alter ego in the books, and there is room to grow. I have known girls to begin reading the series with a special interest in Holly Hollister, only to shift their attention to Pam as they approached her age. The variety in the stereotypes represented by the characters — Pete the leader, Pam the good-hearted, Ricky the mischief-maker, Holly the tomboy, Sue the cute baby — further increases the likelihood that readers will find a particular character to espouse.[20]

Multiple protagonists are the rule in domestic fiction that concerns large families and their adventures together, from Alcott's March family and Margaret Sidney's Five Little Peppers in the nineteenth century to twentieth-century classics like C. S. Lewis's Narnia Chronicles and Madeleine L'Engle's *A Wrinkle in Time* and its sequels. Stratemeyer joined up with this tradition long before the Happy Hollisters were created — the Bobbsey Twins (begun in 1904); the Six Little Bunkers (1918–33); the Four Little Blossoms (1920–30); and the Flyaways (1925), a unique fantasy series about a family that visits the characters found in well-known fairy tales.[21] In a sense the Happy Hollisters series, along with some of these other family adventures, is a juvenile soap opera, one of the comparatively few narrative forms for adults that feature multiple focal characters. It has been argued that the soaps encourage a special allegiance precisely because of their intimate and ongoing presentation of large families from the inside out.[22] This is surely the case in the domestic mysteries about the Hollisters, the difference between the prevailing moods in these two kinds of family stories (accord vs. discord) aside.

Once involved with the characters in domestic drama, the reader or viewer may begin to see fiction as fact. Viewers of soap operas have shown an amazing belief in and loyalty to characters in daytime drama. They send condolence cards and gifts as the fictional situation dictates; if given the opportunity offscreen, they physically assault actresses who play villainesses. While child readers of the Hollisters books have not to my knowledge been so "outspoken," their attachment is of the same sort. As Selma Lanes has commented, by offering "a constantly open window to lives in progress other than one's own," series books such as this one tend to blur the distinction between story and real life.[23]

Earlier it was said that the Happy Hollisters mystery series, with its attention to searching for the hidden, merely magnified the patterns of discovery at work in the majority of children's books and in young childen's reading of those books. The uncovering of some secret or the unraveling of something confusing — that is the direction of children's lives, moreover, as they gain experience and learn about the world. Thus this simplistic mystery series epitomizes the inherent appeal the literature of detection holds for young readers: they instinctively yearn to uncover the hidden. Yet even as the lure of buried treasure leads readers to terra incognita and excites their interest in the novel (and in novel reading), the comforts of home and of sharing countless intimate moments with a perfect family like the Hollisters are also seductive. The animals on the merry-go-round undulate forward, offering an enjoyable ride, but equally enchanting is the lullaby of the sweet and happy music and the pleasure of returning again and again to the same wonderful place.

The Hardy Boys, over the years.

(Three covers from *The Melted Coins*, Franklin W. Dixon; first published by Grosset and Dunlap, 1944.)

8

STRATEMEYER'S SUCCESS
Further Investigation

I am wondering if the [detective story] does not commonly exhibit certain of the very elementary virtues of prose fiction.

—Joseph Wood Krutch

Clues to the reasons behind the spectacular and long-lived success of the Edward Stratemeyer mystery series present themselves as plainly as the fresh footprints in his books, turning up in both the history of his publishing Syndicate and within the pages of the books he and that firm produced. Inside the nearly eighty-year-old enterprise Stratemeyer created there has always been at work a kind of "literary Darwinism," a continuous process of creation, adaptation, and survival of the fittest. A series is begun and, if popular, it embarks on a life of its own. This life may include a host of shifts and new directions in the course of its development. Then there are the offspring spawned by the successful series, a group of distinct but distinctly related series started as soon as a clear winner has been identified. Finally, the Syndicate has shown a willingness to experiment — it has issued a goodly number of deliberate mutants, some of which never made it while others proved tremendously fit . . . and perhaps even sired their own second-generation series.

As much as this pattern of entrepreneurial evolution has contributed to the vitality of the literary house that Edward Stratemeyer built, the unchanging ingredients within the Syndicate novels have determined his mystery series' strong showing. Those behind the conceptualization of the Rover Boys, Ruth Fielding, the Hardy Boys, Nancy Drew, and the Happy Hollisters hit upon characters fairer than all the rest: they had star potential. Then the Syndicate elders designed highly patterned, but very suspenseful plots for their heroes and heroines that immediately tapped readers' own desire to explore and triumph over all they encounter. That is, the Stratemeyer series mysteries have long supplied, and continue to supply, mythic figures who answer to the dreams of American youth culture and to the perennial psychological needs of the young as they set out to discover life's secrets. And the "elementary virtues" of detective novels — specifically the Syndicate's formulaic method of telling its mysteries — have always assured that the Stratemeyer series speak to mass audiences, the most tentative readers included.

Stratmeyer's knack for being on the spot when opportunity knocked has been chronicled in the second chapter. In his personal life and in the publishing arena he was ever ready to follow up a likely prospect. The record of what happened *after* the series discussed in this book proved themselves winners illustrates the Syndicate's well-developed sense of timeliness. The Rover Boys had been on the market only two years when Edward Stratemeyer introduced Arthur M. Winfield's Putnam Hall books about earlier days at Colby Hall, transformed into a military school the second time around. In 1905 he brought out, under his own name, another school series featuring Dave Porter in, as it turned out, fifteen novels. Even as he attempted to corner the market for school adventure series, Stratemeyer continued efforts at writing the other kind of story incipient in the Rover Boys books, the twentieth-century travel adventure. In 1906 he began a soon-to-be best seller, the Motor Boys, and the outdoor adventure series, the Boy Hunters. The fourth volume of the latter series also gives evidence of Stratemeyer's quickness to incorporate the most recent social trends and pastimes into his work in the interest of salability: *Out with a Gun and Camera* "takes up the new fad of photographing wild animals as well as shooting them."[1] In 1907, Jack Ranger appeared, a six-volume series that was a little of everything — school story, sports fiction, big game and yachting adventures. The same can be said of Allen Chapman's Darewell

Chums series, started in 1908, and Frank V. Webster's Webster Series, published from 1909–1915 and embracing twenty-five volumes. And so things went until 1910 when Stratemeyer struck it rich with the technological adventure tales of Tom Swift. All the while, and after, the Rover Boys carried on, and in 1917 a spin-off series about the sons of the first Rovers was born.

The publishing context for Franklin W. Dixon's Hardy Boys is somewhat different. Frank and Joe Hardy were but one of a handful of new series heroes created in the mid-1920s. Between 1925 and 1927 the Syndicate marketed a jungle adventure series (Bomba the Jungle Boy), an explorer adventure series (Don Sturdy), a sports series (the Garry Grayson Football Stories), a western adventure series (James Cody Ferris's X Bar X Boys), the Nat Ridley Rapid Fire Detective Stories, and the Ted Scott flying series — all in addition to the Hardy Boys and to three reissued series.[2] Out of this eclectic group at least one superhit was likely, and Dixon's mystery series was the one, though several of the others fared well, too, especially Ted Scott and Bomba, both of whose series ran to twenty titles. In this midtwenties' burst of Syndicate energy, the method was that of the gardener: a variety of new series was sown, and then the Syndicate waited to see which ones took root.

As for girls' series, the situation was similar. Ruth Fielding first appeared in 1913, and she was one of five new girls' adventure series tried by the Syndicate that year and the next. As explained in an earlier chapter, her stories quickly took on the look of the mystery genre. As soon as this new direction promised to be fruitful, the Syndicate put out other adventure mystery series for girls. Annie Roe Carr's Nan Sherwood stories came into being in 1916, and in 1920 Stratemeyer capitalized on the name of Ruth Fielding's creator by initiating the Betty Gordon series and attributing it to Alice B. Emerson.[3] This moderately successful line — fifteen volumes and a twelve-year history — was one of the first to originate as mystery fiction, as was an interesting series credited to Janet D. Wheeler featuring Billie Bradley.

If the situation around Ruth Fielding's appearance resembles that of the Hardy Boys, Nancy Drew's context looks more like the Rover Boys'. The blonde lawyer's daughter did not premiere amidst a flock of also-rans. Befitting her singular and independent qualities, Nancy was the first new girls' series on the Stratemeyer list since 1926, when May Hollis Barton's Barton Books for Girls, a motley collection of adventure novels without a common heroine, first appeared. Once she established the girl detective as the hottest-selling fictional heroine for young female readers, the Syndicate—much as Stratemeyer himself had done after the Rover Boys' smashing success—followed through with four new girl sleuths: Doris Force in 1931 and the Dana Girls and Kay Tracey in 1934. The latter two series were to become real "breeders," to use the Syndicate's term, themselves; Carolyn Keene's second series about Louise and Jean Dana continued until 1979 (thirty-four volumes). From the beginning the Syndicate actively pushed this series' connection with the Drew books. One advertisement read: "Every girl will love these fascinating stories which tell how the Dana girls, like Nancy Drew herself, meet and match the challenge of each strange new mystery." Frances K. Judd's sixteen-year-old Kay Tracey, though her series was active for only eight years, has exhibited noteworthy lasting power. The eighteen-volume series has had five different reprint publishers, including in the 1980s Bantam Books, which issued six Tracey mysteries in paperback. Some of the titles still in print intimate this series' link with the Gothic mysteries Keene wrote around Nancy Drew: *In the Sunken Garden, The Mansion of Secrets, The Green Cameo Mystery*.

These approaches—copying the clear-cut successes and storming the market with an array of different series—have not, of course, always produced positive results. Doris Force, one of the Drew look-alikes, lasted but two years and four volumes. Similarly, Philip A. Bartlett's four Roy Stover mysteries, issued from 1929–1934, did not ride along on the success of the contemporary Hardy Boys. And when in the 1960s the Syndicate's Andrew Svenson began a family mystery series à la the Hollisters but featuring a black family, it fizzled after the initial three volumes.[4] Some of the experimental series that were part of the "storming-the-market" strategy also died young—for example, many of the sports series, with the exception of Lester Chadwick's Baseball Joe books; the fantasy series written for the youngest readers (Laura Lee Hope's Make-Believe Stories about toys that come to life, the Flyaways by Alice Dale Hardy). Most of the series introduced in the 1960s tended to fall into this category, in fact. For boys, the Bret King western mysteries by "Dan Scott"—actually written, in part, by Svenson—lasted from 1960 to 1964; and Jack Lancer's Christopher Cool/TEEN Agent, the Syndicate's only out-and-out venture into spy fiction, made it through three years and six books.[5] Interestingly, the girls' western mystery that followed Bret King, Ann Sheldon's Linda Craig series, has survived or, more accurately, has been revived. Six volumes written by Harriet Stratemeyer Adams were published by Doubleday between 1962 and 1964. In 1981, Simon and Schuster began reprinting the series and issuing new titles. One of the recent titles is *Phantom of Dark Oaks*, a story full of spiral staircases, a stately plantation, supernatural noises, and the threat of ghosts—Nancy Drew in western drag.[6]

Beyond the spin-off and look-alike series, innovations within its popular series have been undertaken by the Stratemeyer Syndicate. Many terminated series have been reissued, successive printings often taking paperback form. These reissuings, and reprintings in general, have usually been accompanied by new dust jacket or cover art and new illustrations, an updating already discussed in connection with the Hardy Boys and Nancy Drew books. Indeed, when in 1979 Simon and Schuster acquired the rights for all new Hardy Boys and Drew books produced by the Syndicate, it held a competition for illustrators to create a "new concept" for the internationally famous detectives.[7] In 1984 Simon and Schuster actually purchased the Syndicate and immediately announced plans to develop even further their renowned private eyes.

It is not only pictorially that long-running series have been updated. Despite the books' underlying sameness, superficial verbal changes regarding the looks, interests, and circumstances of the Syndicate's supersleuths explain in part their success. New generations of readers have come along and have usually perceived the Syndicate's major detectives as contemporaries and as moving in a "scene" that calls to mind, at least in some of its details, the current one. The Rover Boys become involved in Wall Street action after 1913; Ruth Fielding goes to the war front and becomes a part of the fledgling film industry in the same decade; the Hardys take on investigations for the government (and take up rock music) during the Cold War; and Nancy Drew in 1984 solves a mystery surrounding a professional tennis tournament. And they all drive only the most desirable automobile models of the moment. The Hollisters, in their day, play with the latest toys and leisure-time gadgets.

With three of its hit series the Syndicate has not been content to let new volumes reflect the contemporary culture. Titles in the Bobbsey Twins, the Hardy Boys, and the Nancy Drew series were systematically *rewritten* beginning in 1950. This huge and unprecedented revision project lasted over twenty-five years, from 1950, when the first three Bobbsey Twins books were reworked, to 1977, when the twenty-fourth volume of the Nancy Drew series was issued anew.[8] What induced the Syndicate to take on such a task? First, there was the unpleasant condition that a number of the older titles, which were still in print and selling well, contributed to sustaining racial and ethnic prejudice in their stock presentations of blacks, Jews, Italians, Irish, and other non-WASP groups; Carolyn Keene herself said her books were revised so as "not to offend any ethnic group."[9] But there was also the problem that some of the stories were rapidly showing their age, and so were the heroes and heroines. The contemporary patina just noted evoked an *earlier* era, and that was bad. Thus the copyright pages of revised versions in the Drew series bear this statement: "This new story for today's readers is based on the original of the same title."

The degree and the kind of revision made — and nearly one hundred books were involved — varied considerably. Some new titles are no more than slightly touched-up copies of the original. In Carolyn Keene's *The Clue in the Crumbling Wall*, for example, Florianna has become Juliana Johnson, presumably because the former given name, and its diminutive "Flossie," sounded old-fashioned. Likewise Hector Keep, as Dickensian a label as could be, is now Daniel Hector. After they climb over an iron gate at Heath Castle, George Fayne comments to her chums, "Lucky we wore jeans." Finally, another confinement of the heroine has been added to the plot: an assailant accosts Nancy in her own home (and ties Hannah Gruen to a kitchen chair). Aside from these fairly trivial changes, the mystery remains, word for word, the same.[10]

Other old volumes, however, were virtually discarded. Dixon's *The Flickering Torch Mystery* originated in 1943 as a mystery about an eccentric entomologist, Asa Grable, who developed a species of silkworm only to have some of the valuable worms stolen. In both details and larger design, the 1971 revision has been transformed. The blurb at the beginning of the new *The Flickering Torch Mystery* reads:

> Two unexplainable plane crashes near an airport on the East Coast plunge Frank and Joe Hardy into a bizarre case.
>
> When their famous detective father is called to New York City by a group of insurance companies to investigate air freight thefts at Kennedy International Airport, Mr. Hardy asks Frank and Joe to take over his current case of the suspicious plane accidents.
>
> From the moment Frank and Joe find a radioactive engine in an airplane junkyard, unexpected dangers strike like lightning. Despite the repeated attempts on their lives, the teenage detectives pursue their investigation and make a second startling discovery involving contraband uranium isotopes.[11]

What is more, on the first page of the novel Fenton Hardy walks into his boys' bedroom, "which was vibrating from the sounds of Joe's guitar."

There is still another dimension to the Stratemeyer Syndicate's creative marketing strategies. Its best-selling mystery protagonists have enjoyed life beyond the pages of the mystery novel format they originated and thrive in. They have been visualized outside the book as well as in its illustrations. In 1938 and 1939 Warner Brothers released four Nancy Drew movies starring Bonita Granville as the teen detective, John Litel as Carson Drew, and Frankie Thomas as Ted [sic] Nickerson. *Nancy Drew — Detective* appeared in 1938 and was actually based on *The Password to Larkspur Lane*.[12] The following year three more films came out: *Nancy Drew — Reporter*, *Nancy Drew, Trouble Shooter*, and *Nancy Drew and the Hidden Staircase*. Even though the last film's title echoes that of the second novel in the Drew series,[13] these three films are as reconstructed as some of the "revisions" the Syndicate published. In *Nancy Drew and the Hidden Staircase*, for example, a chauffeur is shot and killed; in *Nancy Drew, Trouble Shooter* the young sleuth accompanies her father on a mission to save an old friend from a murder charge. Murder has no part in Keene's series mysteries.

The Warner Brothers films were well received as B movies go. Reviewers' comments in *Variety* range from "great stuff for the moppets" to "[*Hidden Staircase*] should clean up on matinee trade."[14] The Hardy Boys had somewhat less success in their early video appearances. In the 1950s two Hardy Boys mysteries were serialized on Walt Disney's "The Mickey Mouse Club" television show; Tom Kirk and Tim Considine played the feature roles.[15] Another television series was tried in 1967. *The Mystery of the Chinese Junk* was the novel upon which the pilot for this series was patterned. That pilot aired in September of 1967; no series materialized. But a Saturday morning cartoon series "based on the Hardy Boys mysteries" did come to life on ABC-TV in 1969. (This occurrence, by the way, helps to document the drop in the age of Hardys' fans discussed in chapter 4.)[16]

The most recent visualizations of Stratemeyer mysteries are two hour-long television series begun on ABC in 1977 — "The Hardy Boys Mysteries" starring Shaun Cassidy and Parker Stevenson as Joe and Frank Hardy and "The Nancy Drew Mysteries" with Pamela Martin (and later Janet Louise Jackson) as Nancy Drew. Harriet Stratemeyer Adams once said that for years the Syndicate discouraged television adaptations of its series because those making the video versions did not let her see scripts nor "promise to depict characters faithfully."[17] But Universal Studios and ABC did so agree — Syndicate partner Nancy Axelrad, in fact, served as consultant for the pilot of the Nancy Drew series and weekly scripts were approved by the Syndicate. And this series prospered: there were in all forty-six hours of episodes, developed by Glen A. Larson, which ran for two-and-a-half seasons. Then the series went into syndication and continues to be shown today.

The Hardy Boys episodes, which were originally shown on an alternating schedule along with the Drew mysteries, are certainly reminiscent of the direction the series novels had taken by the 1960s. International espionage plays a major part in the scripts. Recently I saw a show that has Joe and Frank being called in by the Justice Department to work as undercover detectives on a case regarding the potential defection of the teenage daughter of a high-ranking Soviet official. In the midst of their efforts to counter KGB agents, there is a second line of inquiry involving a rock star (played by Ed Byrnes) who has just returned from a concert in Moscow. (In other episodes the Hardys themselves provide the rock 'n' roll.) As for Nancy Drew, she flies an airplane and is definitely a liberated and thoroughly contemporary teen; nonetheless, true to the series fiction, she solves many of her mysteries closer to home. An episode rebroadcast in my area a few months ago depicts Nancy posing as a girl seeking work with a carnival that has just passed through River Heights, in an effort to track down the missing jewelry of two old friends of Carson Drew.

These assorted video adaptations indicate that the Stratemeyer Syndicate has not given in to the film and television industries that have drained off much of the young reading public over the last fifty years with their visual narratives of adventure and mystery. The Syndicate has also taken steps in its own publishing practices to keep its supersleuths as much a part of American popular culture as fast food and video games.

In 1978 the process of translating the Stratemeyer megastars into new media came full circle when Grosset and Dunlap issued two books "Based on the Universal Television Series 'Hardy Boys/Nancy Drew Mysteries' Developed for Television by Glen A. Larson. Based on the Hardy Boys Books by Franklin W. Dixon and the Nancy Drew Books by Carolyn Keene."[18] In fact, the entire decade of the 1970s was a busy one for the Syndicate, which continued publication of its winning series and at the same time began new kinds of spin-offs. In addition to the stories inspired by television scripts, the following were published: *A Super Boy, Super Girl Anthology* (revised edition), *The Hardy Boys' Detective Handbook* (revised edition), *The Nancy Drew Cookbook: Clues to Good Cooking* (including the Detective Burger), *Hardy Boys — Secret Codes*, *Nancy Drew — Detective Logic Puzzles*, two Nancy Drew picture books, and *The Nancy Drew Sleuth Book: Clues to Good Sleuthing*. Since Simon and Schuster began publishing new titles in the five currently vital series, the Hardys and Drew have been written into other newfangled narratives: *The Hardy Boys' Hand-*

book: Seven Stories of Survival, The Hardy Boys' Who-Dunnit Mystery Book, The Nancy Drew Book of Hidden Clues, and a joint venture *Nancy Drew and the Hardy Boys — Super Sleuths!* In 1984 a new type of series was introduced, the "Be a Detective Mystery Stories," again featuring Frank, Joe, and Nancy at work together.

Short stories, puzzle books, picture books for younger readers, an anthology of golden oldies, detective manuals, a cookbook — all suggest the Syndicate's industrious attempts to attract and hold readers' attention. An interesting common denominator in many of these publications is their interactive nature. Readers are urged to participate in the games the Hardys and Nancy Drew play in the books, or in others about the famous detectives. *Hardy Boys — Secret Codes,* for instance, begins with this list of instructions:

- First, read the story. *Read carefully!* There are clues along the way.

- Sometimes you will *decode* secret messages. To decode means to crack, or break, a code message into its regular meaning.

- Sometimes you will *encode* secret messages. To encode means to turn a regular message into code symbols.
    . . .
- If you get stuck, solutions appear at the back of the book.[19]

The new "Be a Detective" line, inspired by the flourishing create-your-own-adventure genre of juvenile books, provides the best example of the level of engagement to which readers are now being urged. Carolyn Keene and Franklin W. Dixon, coauthors of titles in this series, write readers an introductory letter:

Dear Fans,

Since so many of you have written to us saying how much you want to be detectives like Nancy Drew and The Hardy Boys, we figured out a way. Of course, we had to put our heads together to create mysteries that were so baffling they needed help from everyone including Nancy, Frank, Joe and you!

In these exciting new BE A DETECTIVE MYSTERY STORIES you'll be part of a great team of amateur sleuths following clues and wily suspects. At every turn you'll have a chance to pick a different trail filled with adventure that may lead to danger, surprise or an amazing discovery!

The choices are all yours — see how many there are and have fun!

C. K. and F. W. D.[20]

It seems that these latest Syndicate offerings at least implicitly recognize, trendy publishing and marketing techniques notwithstanding, the most fundamental appeal the Stratemeyer mysteries have always contained: readers are in myriad ways drawn to — even pulled into — the workings of their detective idols. Robin Winks has noted that one in four books published in the United States now, aside from required college textbooks, is a murder mystery, detective story, or some hybrid extension of these literary forms; and critics from W. H. Auden to Edmund Wilson have compared adults' appetite for detection to an addiction.[21] The collective loyalty of several generations of young readers to the Stratemeyer Syndicate's series mysteries has been especially fierce. In recapitulation, here are the special secrets and pleasures — the buried treasures — these books contain for readers during their childhood.

"Throughout its [the detective story's] history . . . the detective hero has represented his creator and carried his values into action in society," Ross Macdonald has written.[22] In effect, the Syndicate's eighty-year publishing record has from the first reflected the middle-class assumptions and beliefs of Edward Stratemeyer. Perhaps it is because Stratemeyer, Harriet Stratemeyer Adams, Arthur Svenson, and presumably other Syndicate leaders were so much in the mainstream of American cultural values that their mystery series have spoken to a vast readership. The preferences, ideas, and interests they incorporated into their novels have mirrored those of the populace. Stratemeyer himself, for example, was an enthusiastic automobilist; this enthusiasm underlay the conceptualization of most Syndicate series begun through

1930 (and has been maintained ever since in the ongoing series). Young American readers, whose love affair with the car has continued throughout the century, respond to the freewheeling heroes and heroines Stratemeyer created. To mention a more important cultural connection, the girls' mystery series issued by the Syndicate have more often than not displayed an inherent ambiguity regarding female gender roles. On the one hand, heroines from Ruth Fielding's day on are on the go and accordingly worldly; but on the other, they are polite and respectful of social conventions, distinctly feminine, and very much wrapped up in traditional family patterns of one kind or another. To wit, Nancy Drew is ever daddy's girl even as she demonstrates her independence and sleuthing know-how. Girl readers for three quarters of a century have been caught up in the same two-sided, sometimes tension-producing perspective.

Of course, for Nancy Drew and her sisters there generally is no tension, but instead a harmonious mixture of immediate "social security" and unlimited freedom to escape to and explore the wide world; and this fact hints at the second inherent appeal of the Stratemeyer series mysteries — their psychological value. The perfect heroes and heroines — accomplished, untroubled, sometimes glamorous — always succeed and always in the end get their man. Rational though the investigations in mystery fiction may be, such tales are in their larger vision romantic, as G. K. Chesterton pointed out at the turn of the century.[23] Adults read mysteries in which criminals are exposed and justice triumphs as much to satisfy their human rage for harmony and order as their need to escape mundane circumstances. Children are no different and, what is more, find particular pleasure in stories of young characters who outwit accomplished adult adversaries. Literature of the crafty underdog who bests his "better," from Aesop's fables and Beatrix Potter's tales of Peter Rabbit outlasting Mr. McGregor to Stratemeyer's mysteries, suits their wishes and dreams.

When children pick up a Happy Hollisters, a Hardy Boys, or any other series written about in this book, they do not think of it as a fantasy on the order of *Peter Rabbit*. If they did make the comparison, they would probably put down the mystery, having outgrown their interest in fantasy tales for the time being.[24] But as Margery Fisher rightly observes, adventure stories of the sort that Stratemeyer wrote or authorized, "rest on a delicate balance of fantasy with circumstantial detail."[25] It is that fantastic, or romantic, bedrock — the basic story of the young and the good triumphing over evil — that supplies necessary encouragement and consolation for young readers. In this regard the series mysteries merely pick up where the fairy tales and the fantasy novels to which they have been compared throughout the book leave off.[26]

To the cultural and psychological appeals of Stratemeyer's series mysteries can be added one other kind of pull the books have long exerted on readers, their immense readability. Since the Syndicate's products first took hold of the juvenile reading public, critics, educators, and librarians have been quick to point out that their literary value is nil. This assessment cannot be disputed — it is obvious. But the series mysteries get the highest mark when it comes to readability, which counts, too.

All mystery and detective fiction is, to a greater or lesser degree, formulaic. It is this very quality that can make the genre a straitjacket for many writers, who end up experimenting with, or exploding, the established conventions of detective storytelling. Fredric Jameson has suggested that "genres are essentially contracts between a writer and his readers."[27] Pick up a book called on its cover a "mystery" — or "science fiction" or "western" — and you have a tacit agreement with the author of that book regarding what is to be found within its pages. You know you can make certain assumptions about characterization, action, and even the outcome of the plot based on that one word, "mystery." Inexperienced readers are most likely to think of this preestablished frame of reference as a plus. In the series mysteries the contract is practically signed and sealed. (This is especially true in the Happy Hollisters books, explained elsewhere.) Not only are the story specifications clear, but many of the actual characters and much of the setting are known in advance of opening the book. As Edna Yost said of boys' series books in 1932,

> It's comfortable and easy not to have to get acquainted with new people every time a boy opens the covers of a new book. Much as he loves adventure, he likes his own pal, his own gang, his own old cave to go to.[28]

Thus, as surely as the content and ultimate outcome of Strate-meyer's mysteries provide psychological comfort in their affir-mation of heroic triumph and a universal justice, so the predict-able mode of storytelling reaffirms the readers' hopes that they are up to the task of reading stories.

Sufficiently confident, readers normally decide to play out for themselves the puzzle inside the book. True, some may mere-ly be along for a pleasant ride, but mysteries are stories meant to be engaged in — this is another aspect of the contractual ar-rangement. In a fascinating mystery for children, *Emil and the Detectives*, published in 1929, Erich Kästner includes a prelude to the novel entitled "But the Story Does Not Begin Yet," in which he talks directly to readers explaining how he came to write the novel and asking them to join in the creative process:

> Perhaps you'll be quick enough to make up the story from the
> different parts before I tell it to you? That would be a stunt —
> just as if you were given a pile of building blocks and you had
> to build a station or a church, and you had no plan, and you
> weren't allowed to have one block left over.[29]

What follows, but still precedes the story, are ten sketches — six of characters in the upcoming tale, four of places in which the story is set. Though the building blocks — or puzzle pieces, if you will — are not so demonstratively set forth at the beginning of a Stratemeyer mystery, about the same ingredients are known (unless it is the reader's first encounter with the series), and the comfort of having one's literary bearings is in itself an invitation to discover the unknowns within.

What is the game of construction or discovery like in a series mystery? In a word, elementary, and this is what Joseph Wood Krutch was getting at in his remark quoted at the beginning of this chapter. Mysteries do write large, and thereby exemplify, the "elementary virtues of prose fiction" — namely, careful and intriguing plotting, clear-cut characters whose motives must be figured out and who are in open conflict with one another, a set-ting that must be scrutinized for the clues it provides regarding people and events. To read a rigidly formulaic series mystery is to enroll in a beginners' course in the elements of prose fiction; within the book itself, then, tender readers continue to receive directions for exploring the unknowns of fiction. Mysteries also highlight the reader's obligation, or part, in reading, reading anything. Linguist and reading specialist Frank Smith has called reading "risky business" in that it involves constant guessing or speculation, which we make in order to reduce the welter of confusing alternatives found in a book.[30] In mysteries the game of prediction, the back-and-forth process of guessing what is to come based on what has already been learned, is out in the open. At any point in the reading, readers work from the accumulated evidence they have received through clues to make guesses about the aspects of the case the author is still withholding. The recent interactive follow-ups to Nancy Drew and the Hardy Boys simply *press* the terms of this game.[31]

Smith goes on to say, "If our predictions fail, we are surprised, and if we have nothing to predict because we have no uncertainty, we are bored." The latter is what happens in time to readers of the series mysteries. Having learned by heart the easy-to-spot fictional formulas and having seen the unerring sleuths bedazzle one and all time and again with their serendipitous discoveries, they become bored. First, Happy Hollisters readers move on to the Hardy Boys and/or Nancy Drew; then fans of the Hardys and Drew seek more challenging material outside the series mystery. But readers do not simply abandon those books they once regarded so highly, taking with them only fond memories of their favorite heroes and heroines. They also carry over the confidence gained from stories about successful young discoverers and a literary template — a sense of how stories are constructed and proceed — that will be helpful later. Schooled in the elementary virtues of fiction and having fully discovered all the secrets of the series mysteries for themselves, they are ready, in both senses of the word, to explore what is beyond.

CHECKLIST
Stratemeyer Mystery
and
Adventure Series

The Stratemeyer series listed below are the ones mentioned in the book. Those including at least several mystery novels are asterisked. The list is chronological, but some of the series have been reissued. Dates after the first run indicate this fact.

SERIES	AUTHOR	PUB. DATES
Old Glory	Edward Stratemeyer	1898–1901
* Rover Boys	Arthur M. Winfield	1899–1926
* Putnam Hall	Arthur M. Winfield	1901–1911, 1921
* Bobbsey Twins	Laura Lee Hope	1904–
Dave Porter	Edward Stratemeyer	1905–1919
Deep Sea	Roy Rockwood	1905–1908
Boy Hunters	Captain Ralph Bonehill	1906–1910
* Motor Boys	Clarence Young	1906–1924
Jack Ranger	Clarence Young	1907–1911
* Darewell Chums	Allen Chapman	1908–1911
Dorothy Dale	Margaret Penrose	1908–1924
The Webster Series	Frank V. Webster	1909–1915, 1938
Lakeport	Edward Stratemeyer	1908–1912
* Motor Girls	Margaret Penrose	1910–1917
* Tom Swift	Victor Appleton	1910–1941
Outdoor Chums	Captain Quincy Allen	1911–1916
Baseball Joe	Lester Chadwick	1912–1928

SERIES	AUTHOR	PUB. DATES
Boys of Columbia High	Graham B. Forbes	1912–1920
Up and Doing	Frederick Gordon	1912
Dave Dashaway	Roy Rockwood	1913–1915
* Motion Picture Chums	Victor Appleton	1913–1916
* Moving Picture Boys	Victor Appleton	1913–1922
* Outdoor Girls	Laura Lee Hope	1913–1933
* Ruth Fielding	Alice B. Emerson	1913–1934
Speedwell Boys	Roy Rockwood	1913–1915
Amy Bell Marlowe's Book for Girls	Amy Bell Marlowe	1914–1916, 1933
* Fairview Boys	Frederick Gordon	1914–1917
Girls of Central High	Gertrude W. Morrison	1914–1919
Moving Picture Girls	Laura Lee Hope	1914–1916
* Corner House Girls	Grace Brooks Hill	1915–1926
White Ribbon Boys	Raymond Sperry, Jr.	1915
Bunny Brown and His Sister Sue	Laura Lee Hope	1916–1931
* Nan Sherwood	Annie Roe Carr	1916–1937
* Dave Fearless	Roy Rockwood	1918, 1926–1927
Six Little Bunkers	Laura Lee Hope	1918–1930, 1933
* Betty Gordon	Alice B. Emerson	1920–1932
* Billie Bradley	Janet D. Wheeler	1920–1932
Make-Believe Stories	Laura Lee Hope	1920–1923
Four Little Blossoms	Mabel C. Hawley	1920–1930, 1938
Radio Girls	Margaret Penrose	1922–1924
Honey Bunch	Helen Louise Thorndyke	1923–1955
* Blythe Girls	Laura Lee Hope	1925–1932
* Don Sturdy	Victor Appleton	1925–1935
Flyaways	Alice Dale Hardy	1925
* Barton Books for Girls	May Hollis Barton	1926–1937
Bomba the Jungle Boy	Roy Rockwood	1926–1938, 1953
Frank Allen	Graham B. Forbes	1926–1927
Garry Grayson Football Stories	Elmer A. Dawson	1926–1932
* Movie Boys	Victor Appleton	1926–1927
* Nat Ridley Rapid Fire Detective Stories	Nat Ridley, Jr.	1926–1927
* X Bar X Boys	James Cody Ferris	1926–1942
* Hardy Boys	Franklin W. Dixon	1927–

SERIES	AUTHOR	PUB. DATES
Ted Scott	Franklin W. Dixon	1927–1943
* Roy Stover	Philip A. Bartlett	1929–1934
Campfire Girls	Margaret Penrose	1930
* Nancy Drew	Carolyn Keene	1930–
* Doris Force	Julia K. Duncan	1931–1932
Jerry Ford Wonder Stories	Fenworth Moore	1931–1932, 1937
* Perry Pierce	Clinton W. Locke	1931–1934
* Dana Girls	Carolyn Keene	1934–1979
* Kay Tracey	Frances K. Judd	1934–1942, 1951–1953, 1978, 1980
* Mary and Jerry	Francis Hunt	1935–1937
* Happy Hollisters	Jerry West	1953–1970, 1979
Tom Swift, Jr.	Victor Appleton II	1954–
* Honey Bunch and Norman	Helen Louise Thorndyke	1957–1963
* Bret King	Dan Scott	1960–1964
* Linda Craig	Ann Sheldon	1962–1964, 1981–
* Christopher Cool/ TEEN Agent	Jack Lancer	1967–1969
* Tolliver Adventure Series	Alan Stone	1967

NOTES

1. The Rise of Series Fiction

1. These statistics, and a number of those that follow, come from Deidre Johnson's invaluable reference work: *Stratemeyer Pseudonyms and Series Books: An Annotated Checklist of Stratemeyer and Stratemeyer Syndicate Publications* (Westport, Conn.: Greenwood, 1982).

2. *Under Dewey at Manila; or, The War Fortunes of a Castaway* (Boston: Lee and Shepard, 1898).

3. These translations sometimes rename the heroine; Nancy is "Kitty" in Sweden, "Nerte" in Finland, and "Alice Roy" in France (where she was created by author "Caroline Quine").

4. Arthur M. Winfield, *The Rover Boys Down East; or, The Struggle for the Stanhope Fortune* (New York: Grosset and Dunlap, 1911).

5. Arthur M. Winfield, *The Rover Boys Winning a Fortune; or, Strenuous Days Afloat and Ashore* (New York: Grosset and Dunlap, 1926).

6. Baum wrote other forgotten series — e.g., the Flying Girl Books also under the Van Dyne pseudonym. See Justin G. Schiller, "L. Frank Baum and His Teen-Age Serials: A Bibliographical Checklist," *Boys' Book Collector*, 2 (Spring 1971).

7. The history of Nick Carter publications is retold by Quentin Reynolds, *The Fiction Factory . . . The Story of 100 Years of Publishing at Street and Smith* (New York: Random House, 1955), pp. 39ff. Also, Johnson, *Stratemeyer Pseudonyms*, pp. 63–76.

8. These are the American books for girls, but corresponding English fiction was also read by American girls. The tradition on the other side of the Atlantic is described by Mary Cadogan and Patricia Craig in *"You're*

a brick, Angela!": A New Look at Girls' Fiction from 1839–1975 (London: Victor Gollancz, 1976).

9. These books are among the subjects of Alice M. Jordan's *From Rollo to Tom Sawyer and Other Papers* (Boston: Horn Book, 1948).

10. This point is made as early as 1900. See Everett T. Tomlinson, "Reading for Boys and Girls," *Atlantic Monthly*, 86 (1900), p. 698.

11. The dearth of mainstream fantasy literature in America in the 1800s is explained in Brian Attebery's *The Fantasy Tradition in American Literature* (Bloomington, Ind.: Indiana University Press, 1980). Chapter four concerns children's books.

12. *Adventure, Mystery, and Romance* (Chicago: University of Chicago Press, 1976), pp. 39–40.

13. Like the girls, American boys read British books, too. In the adventure genre there were the stories of G. A. Henty, R. M. Ballantyne, and, of course, Robert Louis Stevenson.

14. Stratemeyer, I repeat, *popularized*, not invented, these kinds of fiction for boys. Noah Brooks, for example, wrote sports books for boys and Jules Verne, science adventures, well before 1900.

15. *The Unembarrassed Muse: The Popular Arts in America* (New York: Dial, 1970), pp. 76–77.

16. Regarding the earlier confinement, see Sandra M. Gilbert and Susan Gubar, *The Madwoman in the Attic* (New Haven: Yale University Press, 1979).

17. *The Delights of Detection* (New York: Criterion Books, 1961), p. 15.

18. *The Pursuit of Crime: Art and Ideology in Detective Fiction* (New Haven: Yale University Press, 1981), p. 50.

19. Those familiar with contemporary reader-response literary criticism will recognize these ideas as those of Wolfgang Iser in *The Implied Reader* (Baltimore: Johns Hopkins University Press, 1974), pp. 274–94.

20. *Down the Rabbit Hole: Adventures and Misadventures in the Realm of Children's Literature* (New York: Atheneum, 1971), p. 128.

2. Edward Stratemeyer: The Man and the Literary Machine

1. "'For It Was Indeed He'." *Fortune*, 9 (April 1934), p. 86.

2. Arthur Prager, "Edward Stratemeyer and His Book Machine," *Saturday Review* (July 10, 1971), p. 53.

3. "Funeral Tonight for E. Stratemeyer," *New York Times* (May 12, 1930), p. 21.

4. The publishing history of these volumes is explained by Deidre Johnson, *Stratemeyer Pseudonyms and Series Books: An Annotated Checklist of Stratemeyer and Stratemeyer Syndicate Publications* (Westport, Conn.: Greenwood, 1982), pp. 5–6.

5. "'For It Was Indeed He'," p. 204.

6. This Preface is taken from the third volume in the series: *The Putnam Hall Champions; or, Bound to Win Out* (New York: Grosset and Dunlap, 1908).

7. This series has been printed and reprinted; its titles have been changed and its volumes, revised. See Johnson, *Stratemeyer Pseudonyms*, pp. 145–47.

8. This and other advertisements quoted elsewhere in my book appeared at the end of the series books; such promotions were common, no matter who the publisher, in the first three decades of the twentieth century.

9. According to Johnson, *Stratemeyer Pseudonyms*, p. xxxv, the Syndicate itself is not sure whether the founding date was 1905 or 1906. The date of incorporation is identified by Peter A. Soderbergh, "Edward Stratemeyer and the Juvenile Ethic, 1894–1930," *International Review of History and Political Science*, 11 (1974), p. 69.

10. See Johnson, *Stratemeyer Pseudonyms*, p. 142.

11. E.g., the Dick Hamilton series, the Mystery Boys series. His son has written a biography, *My Father Was Uncle Wiggily* (New York: McGraw-Hill, 1966).

12. McFarlane writes about his experience with the Syndicate in *Ghost of the Hardy Boys* (New York: Two Continents, 1976).

13. Karen DeWitt, "Nancy Drew's Author—She's No Mystery," *San Antonio* (Texas) *Express-News* (August 7, 1977), pp. 10–11.

14. See Roger B. May, "Durable Heroes: Nancy Drew and Kin Still Surmount Scrapes—and Critics' Slurs," *Wall Street Journal* (January 15, 1975), pp. 1, 17.

15. Johnson, *Stratemeyer Pseudonyms*, pp. xxxi–xxxiii.

16. "'For It Was Indeed He'," p. 89.

17. For the publishing history, see Johnson, *Stratemeyer Pseudonyms*, pp. 129–30.

18. "'For It Was Indeed He'," p. 194.

19. See Judy Klemesrud's interview with Adams: "100 Books—and Not a Hippie in Them," *New York Times* (April 4, 1968), p. 52.

20. Svenson gave several recordings made with his soundscriber, along with drafts and galleys for titles he wrote for the syndicate, to the Lena Y. deGrummond Collection of Children's Literature at the University of Southern Mississippi, Hattiesburg, Mississippi. My account that follows relies on study of these materials.

21. "Tom, Jr.," *New Yorker* (March 20, 1954), p. 26.

22. Quoted in Ed Zuckerman's "The Great Hardy Boys' Whodunit," *Rolling Stone* (September 9, 1976), p. 39.

23. The only reference to murder I have come across in the Syndicate's series is this statement by a friend of the heroine at the outset of Alice B. Emerson's *Betty Gordon on the Campus; or, The Secret in the Trunk Room* (New York: Cupples and Leon, 1928): "Don't mention that woman or I shall commit murder." The speaker's twin replies: "And I might be your accomplice." Nothing comes of the conversation.

24. Tom proposes to Mary Nestor in *Tom Swift and His House on Wheels; or, A Trip to the Mountain of Mystery* (New York: Grosset and Dunlap, 1929), p. 212.

25. Karla Kuskin, "Nancy Drew and Friends," *New York Times Book Review* (May 4, 1975), p. 20.

26. Alice B. Emerson, *Betty Gordon and the Mystery Girl; or, The Secret at Sundown Hall* (New York: Cupples and Leon, 1932).

27. Ann Sheldon, *Linda Craig and the Palomino Mystery* (New York: Doubleday, 1962), p. 95.

28. *The Rover Boys Winning a Fortune; or, Strenuous Days Afloat and Ashore* (New York: Grosset and Dunlap, 1926), p. 176.

29. Edward Stratemeyer, *The Automobile Boys of Lakeport; or, A Run for Fun and Fame* (Boston: Lothrop, Lee and Shepard, 1910), p. 314.

30. Laura Lee Hope, *The Outdoor Girls at Ocean View; or, The Box that Was Found in the Sand* (New York: Grosset and Dunlap, 1915), p. 5.

31. Edward Stratemeyer, *Dave Porter and His Double; or, The Disappearance of the Basswood Fortune* (Boston: Lothrop, Lee and Shepard, 1916), p. 293.

32. Franklin W. Dixon, *Battling the Wind; or, Ted Scott Flying around Cape Horn* (New York: Grosset and Dunlap, 1933), p. 14.

33. Laura Lee Hope, *The Blythe Girls: Rose's Great Problem; or, Face to Face with a Crisis* (New York: Grosset and Dunlap, 1925), p. 1.

34. I noted that in Svenson's revised manuscripts, however, Tom Swifties were often emended, as in the revision of *The Happy Hollisters and the Mystery of the Mexican Idol* discussed earlier.

35. Carolyn Keene, *The Secret of the Old Clock* (New York: Grosset and Dunlap, 1959), p. 21.

36. Quoted by Peter A. Soderbergh, "The Stratemeyer Strain: Educators and the Juvenile Series Book, 1900–1973," *Journal of Popular Culture*, 7 (1974), p. 865.

37. Franklin K. Mathiews, "Blowing Out the Boy's Brains," *Outlook* (November 18, 1914), p. 653.

38. Mrs. Sarah Trimmer, *The Guardian of Education*, 4 (1805), pp. 74–75.

39. See Selma Lanes, *Down the Rabbit Hole: Adventures and Misadventures in the*

Realm of Children's Literature (New York: Atheneum, 1971), chap. 9.

40. Probably the most famous is the *Winnetka Graded Book List*, compiled by Carleton Washburne and Mabel Vogel (Chicago: American Library Association, 1926). This study polled some thirty-six thousand American schoolchildren; it showed that fifth-, sixth-, and seventh-graders' reading was chiefly in the "trashy" Stratemeyer series.

41. L. M. Montgomery, *Anne of Green Gables* (New York: Grosset and Dunlap, 1908), p. 234.

3. The Rover Boys: Suspense at School and on the Road

1. Everett T. Tomlinson, "Reading for Boys and Girls," *Atlantic Monthly*, 86 (1900), pp. 698–99.

2. Other examples are found in Gilbert Patten's Frank Merriwell books and Ralph Henry Barbour's sports fiction; the works of the latter continued for nearly half a century, from 1899–1944.

3. *The Rover Boys at College; or, The Right Road and the Wrong* (New York: Grosset and Dunlap, 1910), p. 229.

4. Edmund Pearson mentions Nick Carter's transitional status in *Dime Novels; or, Following an Old Trail in Popular Literature* (Port Washington, N.Y.: Kennikat Press, 1929) and includes discussion of the first dime novel detectives, Old Cap Collier and the Old Sleuth.

5. *St. Nicholas*, 28 (February 1901), p. 360.

6. Arthur Prager, *Rascals at Large, or, The Clue in the Old Nostalgia* (Garden City, N.Y.: Doubleday, 1971), p. 219.

7. *The Rover Boys in Southern Waters; or, The Deserted Steam Yacht* (1907; rpt. New York: Grosset and Dunlap, 1908), p. 2.

8. Fredric Jameson, "On Raymond Chandler," *The Southern Review*, n.s. 6 (1970), p. 634.

9. *The Rover Boys on Sunset Trail; or, The Old Miner's Mysterious Message* (New York: Grosset and Dunlap, 1925), p. 14.

10. *The Rover Boys Down East; or, The Struggle for the Stanhope Fortune* (New York: Grosset and Dunlap, 1911), p. 12.

11. Until and even after their own mystery and adventure series came along, girls did read boys' books; this *may* account for the attention to courtship in the Rover Boys series.

12. *The Rover Boys in Alaska; or, Lost in the Fields of Ice* (New York: Grosset and Dunlap, 1914), p. 41.

13. Franklin K. Mathiews, "Blowing Out the Boy's Brains," *Outlook* (November 18, 1914), p. 652.

14. A. E. Murch, *The Development of the Detective Novel*, rev. ed. (Westport, Conn.: Greenwood, 1968), p. 140.

15. *The Rover Boys on Land and Sea; or, The Crusoes of Seven Islands* (1903; rpt. New York: Grosset and Dunlap, 1908), p. 159.

16. *The Rover Boys in Business; or, The Search for the Missing Bonds* (New York: Grosset and Dunlap, 1915), p. 250.

17. *The Rover Boys at School; or, The Cadets of Putnam Hall* (1899; rpt. New York: Grosset and Dunlap, 1908), p. 71.

18. *The Rover Boys on the Plains; or, The Mystery of Red Rock* (1906; rpt. New York: Grosset and Dunlap, 1908), p. 123.

19. The entire series can be seen as part of the ongoing middle-class effort to instill manliness and virtue in its youth. See David I. Macleod, *Building Character in the American Boy: The Boy Scouts, YMCA, and Their Forerunners 1870–1920* (Madison, Wisc.: University of Wisconsin Press, 1983).

20. Frank Luther Mott, *Golden Multitudes: The Story of Best Sellers in the United States* (New York: Bowker, 1947), p. 207.

21. William Ruehlmann, *Saint with a Gun: The Unlawful American Private Eye* (New York: New York University Press, 1974), p. 5.

22. G. Stanley Hall, *Adolescence: Its Psychology and Its Relations to Physiology, Anthropology, Sociology, Sex, Crime, Religion, and Education* (New York: Appleton, 1904).

23. *The Anatomy of Criticism* (Princeton: Princeton University Press, 1957), p. 186.

24. Robert Louis Stevenson, *Treasure Island* (Boston: Little, Brown, 1883); James Barrie, *Peter and Wendy* (*Peter Pan*) (New York: Scribner's, 1911); Arthur Ransome, *Swallows and Amazons* (Philadelphia: Lippincott, 1931).

25. *The Rover Boys on Treasure Isle; or, The Strange Cruise on the Steam Yacht* (New York: Grosset and Dunlap, 1909), p. 61.

26. Dennis Porter, *The Pursuit of Crime: Art and Ideology in Detective Fiction* (New Haven: Yale University Press, 1981), p. 108.

4. Ruth Fielding: Orphan Turned Hollywood Sleuth

1. *Girls Series Books: A Checklist of Hardback Books Published 1900–1975*, prepared by the staff of the Children's Literature Research Collections, University of Minnesota (Minneapolis, 1978). It should be noted that this bibliography includes fiction for younger children of both sexes as well as girls' series books.

2. Frank Luther Mott discusses the family novel in the early 1900s in chapter

32 of *Golden Multitudes: The Story Best Sellers in the United States* (New York: Bowker, 1947).

3. *Dorothy Dale, a Girl of Today* (New York: Cupples and Leon, 1908). Interestingly, L. Frank Baum's heroine of the contemporary Oz novels is named Dorothy Gale.

4. The Stratemeyer Syndicate joined the bandwagon late in this area: in 1930 it reprinted Margaret Penrose's four-volume Radio Girls series with new covers and title pages, calling the protagonists the Campfire Girls the second time around.

5. Deidre Johnson, *Stratemeyer Pseudonyms and Series Books: An Annotated Checklist of Stratemeyer and Stratemeyer Syndicate Publications* (Westport, Conn.: Greenwood, 1982), pp. xxiv–xxix.

6. Letter received from Nancy Axelrad, 24 January 1984.

7. Johnson, *Stratemeyer Pseudonyms*, p. 307.

8. *Ruth Fielding and Her Double* (New York: Cupples and Leon, 1932), p. 99.

9. *Ruth Fielding at Cameron Hall; or, A Mysterious Disappearance* (New York: Cupples and Leon, 1928), p. 1.

10. *Bab: A Sub-Deb* (New York: George H. Doran, 1917). First-generation female detectives are surveyed in *Crime on Her Mind*, ed. Michele Slung (New York: Pantheon, 1975).

11. Laura Lee Hope, *The Outdoor Girls at Ocean View; or, The Box that Was Found in the Sand* (New York: Grosset and Dunlap, 1915).

12. Jane L. Stewart, *The Camp Fire Girls at the Seashore; or, Bessie King's Happiness* (New York: Saalfield, 1914).

13. *Ruth Fielding at Briarwood Hall; or, Solving the Campus Mystery* (New York: Cupples and Leon, 1913). This is the only Gothicized title in the Fielding series.

14. Bobbie Ann Mason, *The Girl Sleuth: A Feminist Guide* (Old Westbury, N.Y.: Feminist Press, 1975), p. 107.

15. *Ruth Fielding and Her Greatest Triumph; or, Saving Her Company from Disaster* (New York: Cupples and Leon, 1933).

16. I often thought of Ruth when reading Adrienne Applegarth's essay "Some Observations on Work Inhibitions in Women" in *Female Psychology: Contemporary Psychoanalytic Views*, ed. Harold P. Blum (New York: International University Press, 1977).

17. *Ruth Fielding in the Far North; or, The Lost Motion Picture Company* (New York: Cupples and Leon, 1924), p. 35.

18. Both Ruth and real serial stars like Ruth Roland prided themselves on doing their own stunt work. Coincidentally, the first American *film* serial

appeared the year before the first Ruth Fielding book; and that film, *What Happened to Mary?*, charted another orphan from childhood through marriage!

19. *Ruth Fielding on Cliff Island; or, The Old Hunter's Treasure Box* (New York: Cupples and Leon, 1915), p. 173.

20. *Ruth Fielding at College; or, The Missing Examination Papers* (New York: Cupples and Leon, 1917), p. 3.

21. This literary tradition for American women (though not its adaptation for younger female readers) is the subject of Nina Baym's *Woman's Fiction: A Guide to Novels by and about Women in America, 1820–1870* (Ithaca, N.Y.: Cornell University Press, 1978).

22. *Ruth Fielding and the Gypsies; or, The Missing Pearl Necklace* (New York: Cupples and Leon, 1915), p. 204.

23. *Ruth Fielding in Moving Pictures; or, Helping the Dormitory Fund* (New York: Cupples and Leon, 1916), p. 25.

24. These series concern advertising, flight attending, and nursing, respectively. There were other similar though less popular series that centered on Ruth's line of work, acting — e.g., Helen Dore Boylston's Carol Stage Series published from 1941–46 and Virginia Hughes' Peggy Lane Theatre Stories from the 1960s.

25. The kidnapping of Ruth's child occurs in *Ruth Fielding and Baby June* (New York: Cupples and Leon, 1931). This novel curiously anticipates the kidnapping of Charles Lindbergh, Jr., on March 1, 1932.

26. *Ruth Fielding in Talking Pictures; or, The Prisoners of the Tower* (New York: Cupples and Leon, 1930), p. 208.

27. *Ruth Fielding Clearing Her Name; or, The Rivals of Hollywood* (New York: Cupples and Leon, 1929), p. 2.

28. *Adventure, Mystery, and Romance* (Chicago: University of Chicago Press, 1976), p. 41.

29. "From Salvation to Self-Realization: Advertising and the Therapeutic Roots of the Consumer Culture, 1880–1930," in *The Culture of Consumption*, ed. Richard Wightman Fox and T. J. Jackson Lears (New York: Pantheon, 1983), p. 27.

30. These contemporaries of Ruth Fielding are the subject of Linda S. Levstik's "'I am no lady!': The Tomboy in Children's Fiction," *Children's Literature in Education*, 14 (1983), pp. 14–20.

31. *Ruth Fielding and Her Crowning Victory; or, Winning Honors Abroad* (New York: Cupples and Leon, 1934), p. 208.

32. Kate Douglas Wiggin, *Rebecca of Sunnybrook Farm* (Boston: Houghton Mifflin, 1903), p. 327.

5. The Hardy Boys: Soft-Boiled Detection

1. Russel Nye, *The Unembarrassed Muse: The Popular Arts in America* (New York: Dial, 1970), p. 84.

2. According to Julian Symons, *Mortal Consequences: A History — From the Detective Story to the Crime Novel* (New York: Harper and Row, 1972), p. 111, sales of Van Dine's second book, *The Canary Murder Case*, broke all modern publishing records for detective fiction in 1927.

3. *The Young Book Agent; or, Frank Hardy's Road to Success* (New York: Stitt, 1905). See Deidre Johnson, *Stratemeyer Pseudonyms and Series books: An Annotated Checklist of Stratemeyer and Stratemeyer Syndicate Publications* (Westport, Conn.: Greenwood, 1982), p. 98.

4. Preface to *The Automobile Boys of Lakeport* (Boston: Lothrop, Lee and Shepard, 1910), p. vi.

5. The series, attributed to Nat Ridley, Jr., was The Nat Ridley Rapid Fire Detective Stories, and it was published in 1926 and 1927.

6. *While the Clock Ticked* (New York: Grosset and Dunlap, 1932), p. 13.

7. *Footprints under the Window* (New York: Grosset and Dunlap, 1933), p. 218.

8. *The Simple Art of Murder* (1950; rpt. New York: Ballantine, 1972), p. 16.

9. *The Mystery of the Chinese Junk* (New York: Grosset and Dunlap, 1960), p. 3.

10. *The Shore Road Mystery* (New York: Grosset and Dunlap, 1928), p. 209.

11. *Game Plan for Disaster* (New York: Simon and Schuster/Wanderer Books, 1982), p. 11.

12. These rewards were substantial even in the 1920s — e.g., one thousand dollars in *The Secret of the Old Mill*, fifteen hundred dollars in *The Shore Road Mystery*, five thousand dollars in *The Missing Chums*.

13. *Rascals at Large, or, The Clue in the Old Nostalgia* (Garden City, N.Y.: Doubleday, 1971), pp. 116 ff.

14. *The Mystery of the Spiral Bridge* (New York: Grosset and Dunlap, 1966).

15. See C. G. Jung, *Memories, Dreams, and Reflections*, ed. A. Jaffe and trans. R. and C. Winston (New York: Vintage, 1963), chap. 6.

16. "Reading and Daydreams in Latency: Boy-Girl Differences," *Journal of the American Psychoanalytic Assoc.*, 6 (1958); rpt. in *On Development and Education of Young Children*, ed. Emma N. Plank (New York: Philosophical Library, 1978), p. 243.

17. Prager, *Rascals at Large*, p. 104.

18. New York: Harcourt, Brace, 1935; reviewed by William Rose Benét, *Saturday Review* (November 16, 1935), p. 225. Perhaps the best literary illustration of boys' love of secret hiding places is Howard Pyle's *Men of Iron* (New York: Harpers, 1891).

19. "Murder and the Mean Streets: The Hard-Boiled Detective Novel," 1970; rpt. in *Detective Fiction: Crime and Compromise*, ed. Dick Allen and David Chacko (New York: Harcourt, Brace, Jovanovich, 1974), p. 412.

20. *The Twisted Claw* (New York: Grosset and Dunlap, 1939), p. 7.

21. The Jerry Todd books from the late 1920s and early 1930s were written by Edward Edson Lee under the pen name Leo Edwards.

22. *Place in Fiction*, quoted by Eleanor Cameron in her essay "A Country of the Mind," *The Green and Burning Tree* (Boston: Little, Brown, 1962), p. 202.

23. See Erik H. Erikson, *Childhood and Society*, 2nd ed. (New York: Norton, 1963), pp. 262–63.

24. Ed Zuckerman, "The Great Hardy Boys' Whodunit," *Rolling Stone* (September 9, 1976), p. 38.

25. J. M. Barrie, *Peter and Wendy* (*Peter Pan*) (1911; rpt. New York: Bantam, 1981), p. 132.

26. John Gardner, "Learning from Disney and Dickens," *New York Times Book Review* (January 30, 1983), p. 3; Edna Yost, "The Fifty Cent Juveniles," *Publishers Weekly* (June 18, 1932), p. 2408.

27. Telephone interview with Diane Arico, Assistant to the Editor, Simon and Schuster/Wanderer Books, 30 January 1984.

28. Regarding this topic, see David Elkind, *The Hurried Child: Growing Up Too Fast Too Soon* (Reading, Mass.: Addison-Wesley, 1981).

29. E.g., the novels by Robert Cormier, especially *I Am the Cheese* (New York: Pantheon, 1977) and *After the First Death* (New York: Pantheon, 1979).

30. The Hardys, in contrast, "sweat . . . over the ablative absolute." See *The Secret of the Old Mill* (New York: Grosset and Dunlap, 1927), p. 33.

31. This argument is made concerning the fairy tales, themselves full of violent acts, by Bruno Bettelheim, *The Uses of Enchantment* (New York: Knopf, 1976).

6. Nancy Drew: Gothic Detection

1. Recent titles are published by Simon and Schuster in their Wanderer Books line. *Enemy Match* and *The Mysterious Image*, which came out in 1984, introduced a new assistant to Nancy, Midge Watson.

2. *The Clue in the Old Album* (New York: Grosset and Dunlap, 1947), p. 5.

3. Letter received from Nancy Axelrad, 24 January 1984.

4. Some libraries, however, do not let the series circulate. While researching this chapter at the Free Library of Philadelphia, I was told by one of the children's librarians that they did not circulate books "written by committee."

5. Chester Drew appears in *The Blythe Girls: Rose's Great Problem; or, Face to Face with a Crisis* (New York: Grosset and Dunlap, 1925) by Laura Lee Hope.

6. The Dana Girls and Kay Tracey were Stratemeyer efforts and were originally published by Grosset and Dunlap and Cupples and Leon, respectively. Margaret Sutton's Judy Bolton series was also published by Grosset and Dunlap, as was the Cherry Ames series created by Helen Wells. Whitman Publishing Company issued The Trixie Belden Library.

7. These detectives are discussed in the sixth chapter of Patricia Craig and Mary Cadogan's excellent book *The Lady Investigates: Women Detectives and Spies in Fiction* (London: Victor Gollancz, 1981).

8. Quoted by Karen DeWitt, "Nancy Drew's Author—She's No Mystery," *San Antonio* (Texas) *Express-News* (August 7, 1977), pp. 10–11.

9. "Their Success Is No Mystery," *TV Guide* (June 25, 1977), p. 14.

10. *The Clue in the Crumbling Wall* (New York: Grosset and Dunlap, 1945), p. 3.

11. *Clue in the Ancient Disguise* (New York: Simon and Schuster/Wanderer Books, 1982).

12. *The Mystery of the Ivory Charm* (New York: Grosset and Dunlap, 1936), p. 15.

13. Craig and Cadogan, *The Lady Investigates*, p. 155.

14. *The Clue in the Diary* (New York: Grosset and Dunlap, 1932), p. 179.

15. *The Secret of the Forgotten City* (New York: Grosset and Dunlap, 1975), p. 172.

16. *The Ghost of Blackwood Hall* (New York: Grosset and Dunlap, 1948), p. 7.

17. *The Secret in the Old Attic* (New York: Grosset and Dunlap, 1944), p. 50.

18. "Tom, Jr.," *New Yorker* (March 20, 1954), p. 26.

19. *The Girl Sleuth: A Feminist Guide* (Old Westbury, N.Y.: Feminist Press, 1975), chap. 5.

20. *The Mystery of the Glowing Eye* (New York: Grosset and Dunlap, 1974), p. 4.

21. *The Clue of the Dancing Puppet* (New York: Grosset and Dunlap, 1962), p. 172.

22. *The Clue of the Broken Locket* (New York: Grosset and Dunlap, 1934), p. 15.

23. On this point see Joseph F. Kett, *Rites of Passage: Adolescence in America, 1790 to the Present* (New York: Basic Books, 1977), p. 262.

24. The essay appears in Otto Penzler's collection *The Great Detectives* (New York: Penguin, 1978), pp. 82–84 (quote, p. 83).

25. Instead, the young women in the book work off extra energy through constant eating. In *The Mystery of the Tolling Bell* (New York: Grosset and Dunlap, 1946), p. 6, they stop their sleuthing for the largest "snack" on record: puffed shrimp, fried clams, tomatoes, cabbage salad, potatoes, hot biscuits, lemonade, and apple pie. The oral gratification in this series is

discussed by Lee Zacharias, "Nancy Drew, Ballbuster," *Journal of Popular Culture*, 9 (1976), pp. 1027–38.

26. *The Sign of the Twisted Candles* (New York: Grosset and Dunlap, 1933), pp. 2–3.

27. DeWitt, "Nancy Drew's Author—She's No Mystery," p. 10-H.

28. This aspect of the series is considered fully by James P. Jones, "Nancy Drew, WASP Super Girl of the 1930's," *Journal of Popular Culture*, 6 (1973), pp. 707–17.

29. Nancy is called a "true daughter of the Middle West" in *The Secret of the Old Clock* (New York: Grosset and Dunlap, 1930), p. 26.

30. *Rascals at Large, or, The Clue in the Old Nostalgia* (Garden City, N.Y.: Doubleday, 1971), p. 76.

31. I have found two suggestions of Oz actually written into the series. First, Nancy's dog is named Togo—Dorothy's was Toto. Second, in *The Clue in the Jewel Box* (New York: Grosset and Dunlap, 1943) the impostor Nancy unmasks is Francis Baum; the Oz books were written by L. Frank Baum.

32. In their other book, Craig and Cadogan compare the emotional effect of reading a Nancy Drew book to "the feeling of being driven along in a very fast car. Dramatic incidents are over almost before the reader is aware of what is happening." See *"You're a brick, Angela!": A New Look at Girls' Fiction from 1839–1975* (London: Victor Gollancz), p. 305.

33. Rinehart's Gothic mysteries are explored by Jan Cohn, *Improbable Fiction: The Life of Mary Roberts Rinehart* (Pittsburgh, Pa.: University of Pittsburgh Press, 1980).

34. This version was written by Madame Leprince de Beaumont and appeared in her *Magasin des enfans* in London in 1756; the English translation, *The Young Misses Magazine*, was published in 1761.

35. Patricia Meyer Spacks notes the "specifically adolescent female experience" in Gothic fiction in *The Adolescent Idea: Myths of Youth and the Adult Imagination* (New York: Basic Books, 1981), chap. 5.

36. Craig and Cadogan, *The Lady Investigates*, p. 150.

37. Thirty-one years after Hitchcock's *39 Steps* was released Carolyn Keene wrote a Nancy Drew volume whose title evokes that film: *The Mystery of the 99 Steps* (New York: Grosset and Dunlap, 1966).

38. See Jane Ginsburg, "And Then There Is Good Old Nancy Drew," *Ms.* (January 1974), pp. 93–94.

39. *The Girl Sleuth*, p. 74.

40. "Women, Success, and Nancy Drew," *Vogue* (May 1980), p. 324. Regarding what readers pick up after Nancy Drew, see G. Robert Carlsen, *Books and the Teenage Reader*, rev. ed. (New York: Harper and Row, 1980), chap. 3.

7. The Happy Hollisters: Mystery for the Entire Family

1. E.g., *The Bobbsey Twins Treasure Hunting* (New York: Grosset and Dunlap, 1929) and *The Bobbsey Twins' Wonderful Secret* (New York: Grosset and Dunlap, 1931).
2. In the 1960s the revised versions of the first Bobbsey Twins books were also retitled; the new titles usually contained the word *mystery*. Occasionally *adventure* or *secret* was used.
3. The Honey Bunch and Norman series contains twelve volumes and was published from 1957 to 1963; some of the books are reprints of Thorndyke's earlier Honey Bunch novels.
4. Andrew Svenson, Letter to Lena Y. deGrummond, 31 June 1968, Lena Y. deGrummond Collection of Children's Literature, University of Southern Mississippi, Hattiesburg, Mississippi.
5. *The Happy Hollisters at Sea Gull Beach* (Garden City, New York: Garden City Books, 1953). Garden City Books was the original publisher of the first nineteen volumes in the series; Doubleday, of volumes 20 through 33. Doubleday and Grosset and Dunlap are the reprint publishers.
6. *The Happy Hollisters and the Cuckoo Clock Mystery* (Garden City, New York: Doubleday, 1963); *The Happy Hollisters and the Swiss Echo Mystery* (Garden City, New York: Doubleday, 1963).
7. *The Happy Hollisters and the Mystery of the Golden Witch* (Garden City, New York: Doubleday, 1966).
8. *The Happy Hollisters* (Garden City, New York: Garden City Books, 1953), p. 130. Hamilton illustrated all thirty-three volumes in the series, and each title promised on its dust jacket "over seventy illustrations."
9. *The Happy Hollisters and the Mystery in Skyscraper City* (Garden City, New York: Garden City Books, 1959), p. 183.
10. Projected page lengths are penciled in, for example, in the typescript of *The Happy Hollisters and the Mystery of the Mexican Idol* (Garden City, New York: Doubleday, 1967). This material is in the deGrummond Collection at the University of Southern Mississippi.
11. *The Happy Hollisters and the Whistle-Pig Mystery* (Garden City, New York: Doubleday, 1964).
12. *The Happy Hollisters at Lizard Cove* (Garden City, New York: Garden City Books, 1957), pp. 174–75.
13. *The Happy Hollisters and the Secret of the Lucky Coins* (Garden City, New York: Doubleday, 1962), p. 157.
14. *The Happy Hollisters and the Scarecrow Mystery* (Garden City, New York: Garden City Books, 1957), pp. 57–58.

15. "Family Romances," 1909; rpt. *The Complete Works of Sigmund Freud*, trans. James Strachey (London: Hogarth, 1959), Vol. 19, pp. 235–41.

16. The Hollisters are, however, clearly students — they attend Lincoln School throughout the series. *The Happy Hollisters at Snowflake Camp* (Garden City, New York: Garden City Books, 1954) even features their teacher, Miss Nelson, and her missing brother.

17. Kenneth Grahame, *The Wind in the Willows* (1908; rpt. New York: Scribner's, 1961); L. Frank Baum, *The Wonderful Wizard of Oz* (1900; rpt. New York: Dover, 1960), p. 261.

18. *The Girl Sleuth: A Feminist Guide* (Old Westbury, N.Y.: Feminist Press, 1975), chap. 3.

19. *The Happy Hollisters on a River Trip* (Garden City, New York: Garden City Books, 1953), p. 94.

20. In fact, few boys read the Happy Hollisters. As Russel Nye (*The Unembarrassed Muse: The Popular Arts in America* [New York: Dial, 1970], p. 78) asked, "what boy wanted to be caught with the Bobbseys?" The same applies here according to my own and librarians' observations.

21. There were also, of course, all the series with two siblings as protagonists — e.g., the Hardy Boys and the Dana Girls.

22. See Tania Modleski, *Loving with a Vengeance: Mass-Produced Fantasies for Women* (Hamden, Conn.: Shoe String/Archon, 1982), chap. 4.

23. *Down the Rabbit Hole: Adventures and Misadventures in the Realm of Children's Literature* (New York: Atheneum, 1971), p. 128.

8. Stratemeyer's Success: Further Investigation

1. Captain Ralph Bonehill, *Out with Gun and Camera; or, The Boy Hunters in the Mountains* (New York: Cupples and Leon, 1910).

2. Frank Allen, Dave Fearless, and the Movie Boys were the reissued series; all three, as well as the new Nat Ridley stories, were published monthly in paperback editions in 1926 and 1927.

3. Other pseudonyms were especially useful in this respect — e.g., Laura Lee Hope, Victor Appleton, Roy Rockwood, each of whom was credited with at least five series.

4. The Tolliver Adventure Series by Alan Stone. The three volumes all appeared in 1967.

5. Publicity deemed his series "for all mystery-spy fans . . . a suspense thriller packed with pulse-pounding excitement that never lets up till the final paragraph." TEEN, incidentally, stands for Top-secret Educational Espionage Network, and the series takes off from the moment when Chris's

father, Dr. Jonathan Cool, America's "foremost brain in high-energy physics," disappears at a scientific conference.

6. Ann Sheldon, *Phantom of Dark Oaks* (New York: Simon and Schuster/ Wanderer Books, 1984).

7. See Daisy Maryles, "Venerable Young Sleuths Find New Home," *Publishers Weekly* (March 5, 1979), p. 18.

8. *The Clue in the Old Album* was originally published in 1947, exactly thirty years before the revision.

9. Actually these are the words of Harriet Stratemeyer Adams, writing under her pen name, in *The Great Detectives*, ed. Otto Penzler (New York: Penguin, 1978), p. 82.

10. *The Clue in the Crumbling Wall* (New York: Grosset and Dunlap, 1973).

11. *The Flickering Torch Mystery* (New York: Grosset and Dunlap, 1971).

12. Carolyn Keene, *The Password to Larkspur Lane* (New York: Grosset and Dunlap, 1933).

13. Carolyn Keene, *The Hidden Staircase* (New York: Grosset and Dunlap, 1930).

14. "Nancy Drew — Reporter," *Variety* (March 2, 1939); "Nancy Drew and the Hidden Staircase," *Variety* (November 9, 1939).

15. Dell published four comic books based on Dixon's mysteries at about the same time.

16. The intricate history of auxiliary Hardy Boys publications is set forth by Deidre Johnson, *Stratemeyer Pseudonyms and Series Books: An Annotated Checklist of Stratemeyer and Stratemeyer Syndicate Publications* (Westport, Conn.: Greenwood, 1982), pp. 99–100.

17. "Their Success Is No Mystery," *TV Guide* (June 25, 1977), p. 16.

18. *The Hardy Boys and Nancy Drew Meet Dracula* and *The Haunted House and Flight to Nowhere*; the latter includes two stories based on two shows.

19. *Hardy Boys — Secret Codes* by Evan Morley (New York: Stratemeyer Syndicate/Tempo Books, 1977).

20. The four initial titles in the "Be a Detective Mystery Stories" series are: *The Secret of the Knight's Sword, Danger on Ice, The Feathered Serpent,* and *Secret Cargo.*

21. Robin Winks, *Modus Operandi: An Excursion into Detective Fiction* (Boston: Godine, 1982), p. 7; W. H. Auden, "The Guilty Vicarage" in *The Dyer's Hand and Other Essays* (New York: Random House, 1948), pp. 146–58; Edmund Wilson, "Who Cares Who Killed Roger Ackroyd?" in *Classics and Commercials: A Literary Chronicle of the Forties* (New York: Farrar, Straus, Giroux, 1950), pp. 257–65.

22. "The Writer as Detective Hero" in *On Crime Writing* (Santa Barbara, California: Capra, 1973), p. 9.

23. "A Defence of Detective Stories" from *The Defendant* (London: J. M. Dent, 1907), pp. 118–23.

24. On children's loss of appetite for fantasy literature, see Arthur Applebee, *The Child's Concept of Story* (Chicago: University of Chicago Press, 1978), and F. André Favat, *Child and Tale: The Origins of Interest* (Urbana, Ill.: National Council of Teachers of English, 1977).

25. *Intent upon Reading: A Critical Appraisal of Modern Fiction for Children*, rev. ed. (London: Hodder and Stoughton, 1964), p. 251.

26. J. R. R. Tolkien looks at the psychological and imaginative benefits of the fairy tales in "On Fairy Stories" in *Tree and Leaf* (Boston: Houghton Mifflin, 1965).

27. "Magical Narrative: Romance as Genre," *New Literary History*, 7 (1975), p. 135.

28. "The Fifty Cent Juveniles," *Publishers Weekly* (June 18, 1932), p. 2408.

29. *Emil and the Detectives*, trans. May Massee (New York: Doubleday, 1930).

30. *Understanding Reading: A Psycholinguistic Analysis of Reading and Learning to Read*, 2nd ed. (New York: Holt, Rinehart and Winston, 1978), p. 67.

31. See my article, "The Child Reader as Sleuth," *Children's Literature in Education*, 15 (Spring 1984), pp. 30–41.

BIBLIOGRAPHY

Adams, Harriet. "Their Success Is No Mystery." *TV Guide*, 25 June 1977, pp. 13-14, 16.

Applebee, Arthur. *The Child's Concept of Story*. Chicago: University of Chicago Press, 1978.

Applegarth, Adrienne. "Some Observations on Work Inhibitions in Women." In *Female Psychology*. Ed. Harold P. Blum. New York: International Universities Press, 1977, pp. 251-68.

Attebery, Brian. *The Fantasy Tradition in American Literature: From Irving to LeGuin*. Bloomington, Ind.: Indiana University Press, 1980.

Auden, W. H. "The Guilty Vicarage." In *The Dyer's Hand and Other Essays*. New York: Random House, 1948, pp. 146-58.

Bargainnier, Earl F., ed. *Ten Women of Mystery*. Bowling Green, Ohio: Bowling Green State University Popular Press, 1981.

Barzun, Jacques. *The Delights of Detection*. New York: Criterion Books, 1961.

Baym, Nina. *Woman's Fiction: A Guide to Novels by and about Women in America, 1820-1870*. Ithaca, NY: Cornell University Press, 1978.

Benét, William Rose. Review of *The Cave Mystery*, by S. S. Smith. *Saturday Review*, 16 November 1935, pp. 220 ff.

Bettelheim, Bruno. *The Uses of Enchantment: The Meaning and Importance of Fairy Tales*. New York: Knopf, 1976.

Billman, Carol. "The Child Reader as Sleuth." *Children's Literature in Education*, 15 (1984), pp. 30-41.

Blanck, Jacob. *Peter Parley to Penrod: A Bibliographical Description of the Best-Loved American Juvenile Books*. New York: Bowker, 1956.

"Books and Reading for Young Folk." *St. Nicholas*, February 1901, p. 360.

177

Cadogan, Mary, and Patricia Craig. *The Lady Investigates: Women Detectives and Spies in Fiction.* London: Victor Gollancz, 1981.

———. *"You're a brick, Angela!": A New Look at Girls' Fiction from 1839–1975.* London: Victor Gollancz, 1976.

Cameron, Eleanor. *The Green and Burning Tree.* Boston: Little, Brown, 1962.

Carlsen, G. Robert. *Books and the Teenage Reader.* Rev. ed. New York: Harper and Row, 1980.

Cawelti, John. *Adventure, Mystery, and Romance: Formula Stories as Popular Art and Culture.* Chicago: University of Chicago Press, 1976.

Chandler, Raymond. "The Simple Art of Murder." In *The Simple Art of Murder.* 1950; rpt. New York: Ballantine, 1972, pp. 1–21.

Chesterton, G. K. "A Defence of Detective Stories." In *The Defendant.* London: J. M. Dent, 1907, pp. 118–23.

Cohn, Jan. *Improbable Fiction: The Life of Mary Roberts Rinehart.* Pittsburgh: University of Pittsburgh Press, 1980.

DeWitt, Karen. "Nancy Drew's Author—She's No Mystery." *San Antonio* (Texas) *Express-News,* 7 August 1977, pp. 10-H and 11-H.

Dizer, John T., Jr. *Tom Swift and Company: "Boys' Books" by Stratemeyer and Others.* London: McFarland, 1982.

Donelson, Ken. "Nancy, Tom and Assorted Friends in the Stratemeyer Syndicate Then and Now." *Children's Literature,* 7 (1978), pp. 17–44.

Elkind, David. *The Hurried Child: Growing Up Too Fast Too Soon.* Reading, Mass.: Addison-Wesley, 1981.

Erikson, Erik H. *Childhood and Society.* 2nd ed. New York: Norton, 1963.

Favat, F. André. *Child and Tale: The Origins of Interest.* Urbana, Ill.: National Council of Teachers of English, 1977.

Fisher, Margery. *Intent upon Reading: A Critical Appraisal of Modern Fiction for Children.* Rev. ed. London: Hodder and Stoughton, 1964.

Fitzgerald, Frances. "Women, Success, and Nancy Drew." *Vogue,* May 1980, pp. 323–24.

"'For It Was Indeed He'." *Fortune,* April 1934, pp. 86–90 ff.

Freud, Sigmund. "Family Romances." In *The Complete Works of Sigmund Freud.* Trans. James Strachey. Vol. 19. London: Hogarth, 1959.

Frye, Northrop. *The Anatomy of Criticism.* Princeton: Princeton University Press, 1957.

"Funeral Tonight for E. Stratemeyer." *New York Times,* 12 May 1930, p. 21.

Gardner, John. "Learning from Disney and Dickens." *New York Times Book Review,* 30 January 1983, pp. 3, 22–23.

Garis, Roger. *My Father Was Uncle Wiggily.* New York: McGraw-Hill, 1966.

Gilbert, Sandra M. and Susan Gubar. *The Madwoman in the Attic: The Woman Writer and the Nineteenth-Century Literary Imagination.* New Haven: Yale University Press, 1979.

Ginsburg, Jane. "And Then There Is Good Old Nancy Drew." *Ms.*, January 1974, pp. 93-94.

Girls Series Books: A Checklist of Hardback Books Published 1900-1975. Children's Literature Research Collections. University of Minnesota. Minneapolis, 1978.

Goodstone, Tony, ed. *The Pulps.* New York: Chelsea House, 1976.

Grella, George. "Murder and the Mean Streets: The Hard-Boiled Detective Novel." 1970; rpt. in *Detective Fiction: Crime and Compromise.* Ed. Dick Allen and David Chacko. New York: Harcourt, Brace, Jovanovich, 1974, pp. 411-429.

Hall, G. Stanley. *Adolescence: Its Psychology and Its Relation to Physiology, Anthropology, Sociology, Sex, Crime, Religion, and Education.* New York: Appleton, 1904.

Hudson, Harry K. *A Bibliography of Hard-Cover Boys' Books.* Rev. ed. Tampa: Data Print, 1977.

Iser, Wolfgang. *The Implied Reader.* Baltimore: Johns Hopkins University Press, 1974.

Jackson, Jacqueline, and Phillip Kendall. "What Makes a Bad Book Good: *Elsie Dinsmore.*" *Children's Literature*, 7 (1978), pp. 45-67.

Jameson, Fredric. "Magical Narrative: Romance as Genre," *New Literary History*, 7 (1975), 135-63.

———. "On Raymond Chandler." *The Southern Review*, n.s. 6 (1970), pp. 624-50.

Johannsen, Albert. *The House of Beadle and Adams and its Dime and Nickel Novels.* 3 vols. Norman, Oklahoma: University of Oklahoma Press, 1950-1962.

Johnson, Deidre. *Stratemeyer Pseudonyms and Series Books: An Annotated Checklist of Stratemeyer and Stratemeyer Syndicate Publications.* Westport, Conn.: Greenwood, 1982.

Jones, James P. "Nancy Drew, WASP Super Girl of the 1930's." *Journal of Popular Culture*, 6 (1973), pp. 707-17.

Jordan, Alice M. *From Rollo to Tom Sawyer and Other Papers.* Boston: Horn Book, 1948.

Jung, C. G. *Memories, Dreams, and Reflections.* Ed. A. Jaffe and trans. R. and C. Winston. New York: Vintage, 1963.

Kelly, R. Gordon. *Mother Was a Lady: Self and Society in Selected American Children's Periodicals 1865-1890.* Westport, Conn.: Greenwood, 1974.

Kett, Joseph F. *Rites of Passage: Adolescence in America, 1790 to the Present.* New York: Basic Books, 1977.

Klemesrud, Judy. "100 Books — and Not a Hippie in Them." *New York Times*, 4 April 1968, p. 52.

Knoepflmacher, U. C. "Little Girls without Their Curls: Female Aggression in Victorian Children's Literature." *Children's Literature*, 11 (1983), pp. 14–31.

Knox, Caroline. "Nancy Drew." *Poetry*, 137 (1980), p. 155.

Kuskin, Karla. "Nancy Drew and Friends." *New York Times Book Review*, 4 May 1975, pp. 20–21.

Lanes, Selma G. *Down the Rabbit Hole: Adventures and Misadventures in the Realm of Children's Literature*. New York: Atheneum, 1971.

Lears, T. J. Jackson. "From Salvation to Self-Realization: Advertising and the Therapeutic Roots of the Consumer Culture, 1880–1930." In *The Culture of Consumption*. Ed. Richard Wightman Fox and T. J. Jackson Lears. New York: Pantheon, 1983, pp. 1–38.

Levstik, Linda S. "'I am no lady!': The Tomboy in Children's Fiction." *Children's Literature in Education*, 14 (1983), pp. 14–20.

Macdonald, Ross. "The Writer as Detective Hero." In *On Crime Writing*. Santa Barbara, California: Capra Press, 1973, pp. 9–24.

Macleod, David I. *Building Character in the American Boy: The Boy Scouts, YMCA, and Their Forerunners, 1870–1920*. Madison, Wisconsin: University of Wisconsin Press, 1983.

Maryles, Daisy. "Venerable Young Sleuths Find New Home." *Publishers Weekly*, 5 March 1979, p. 18.

Mason, Bobbie Ann. *The Girl Sleuth: A Feminist Guide*. Old Westbury, New York: Feminist Press, 1975.

Mathiews, Franklin K. "Blowing Out the Boy's Brains." *Outlook*, 18 November 1914, pp. 652–54.

May, Roger B. "Durable Heroes: Nancy Drew and Kin Still Surmount Scrapes — and Critics' Slurs." *Wall Street Journal*, 15 January 1975, pp. 1, 17.

McFarlane, Leslie. *Ghost of the Hardy Boys*. New York: Two Continents, 1976.

Modleski, Tania. *Loving with a Vengeance: Mass-Produced Fantasies for Women*. New York: Archon, 1982.

Mott, Frank Luther. *Golden Multitudes: The Story of Best Sellers in the United States*. New York: Bowker, 1947.

Murch, A. E. *The Development of the Detective Novel*. Rev. ed. New York: Greenwood, 1968.

Nancy Drew and the Hidden Staircase. Variety, 9 November 1939.

Nancy Drew — Detective. Variety, 7 December 1938.

Nancy Drew — Reporter. Variety, 2 March 1939.

Nancy Drew, Trouble Shooter. Variety, 20 September 1939.

Nye, Russel B. *The Unembarrassed Muse: The Popular Arts in America*. New York: Dial, 1970.

Pearson, Edmund. *Dime Novels; or, Following an Old Trail in Popular Literature*. Port Washington, New York: Kennikat Press, 1929.

Peller, Lili E. "Reading and Daydreams in Latency: Boy-Girl Differences." 1958; rpt. in *On Development and Education of Young Children*. Ed. Emma N. Plank. New York: Philosophical Library, 1978, pp. 240-43.

Penzler, Otto, ed. *The Great Detectives*. New York: Penguin, 1978.

Porter, Dennis. *The Pursuit of Crime: Art and Ideology in Detective Fiction*. New Haven: Yale University Press, 1981.

Prager, Arthur. "Edward Stratemeyer and His Book Machine." *Saturday Review*, 10 July 1971, pp. 15-17, 52-53.

————. *Rascals at Large, or, The Clue in the Old Nostalgia*. Garden City, New York: Doubleday, 1971.

Reynolds, Quentin. *The Fiction Factory; or, From Pulp Row to Quality Street: The Story of 100 Years of Publishing at Street and Smith*. New York: Random House, 1955.

Ruehlmann, William. *Saint with a Gun: The Unlawful American Private Eye*. New York: New York University Press, 1974.

Ruhm, Herbert, ed. *The Hard-Boiled Detective: Stories from* Black Mask *Magazine, 1920-1951*. New York: Vintage, 1977.

Schiller, Justin G. "L. Frank Baum and His Teen-Age Serials: A Bibliographical Checklist." *Boys' Book Collector*, 2 (1971).

Slung, Michele, ed. *Crime on Her Mind: 15 Stories of Female Sleuths from the Victorian Era to the Forties*. New York: Pantheon, 1975.

Smith, Frank. *Understanding Reading: A Psycholinguistic Analysis of Reading and Learning to Read*. 2nd ed. New York: Holt, Rinehart and Winston, 1978.

Smith, Henry Nash. *Virgin Land: The American West as Symbol and Myth*. Cambridge, Mass.: Harvard University Press, 1950.

Soderbergh, Peter A. "Edward Stratemeyer and the Juvenile Ethic, 1894-1930." *International Review of History and Political Science*, 11 (1974), pp. 61-71.

————. "The Stratemeyer Strain: Educators and the Juvenile Series Book, 1900-1973." *Journal of Popular Culture*, 7 (1974), pp. 864-72.

Spacks, Patricia Meyer. *The Adolescent Idea: Myths of Youth and the Adult Imagination*. New York: Basic Books, 1981.

Symons, Julian. *Mortal Consequences: A History — From the Detective Story to the Crime Novel*. New York: Harper and Row, 1972.

Tolkien, J. R. R. "On Fairy Stories." In *Tree and Leaf*. Boston: Houghton Mifflin, 1965.

"Tom, Jr." *New Yorker*, 20 March 1954, pp. 26–27.

Tomlinson, Everett T. "Reading for Boys and Girls." *Atlantic Monthly*, 86 (1900), pp. 693–99.

Trimmer, (Mrs.) Sarah. *The Guardian of Education*, 4 (1805), pp. 74–75.

Wilson, Edmund. "Who Cares Who Killed Roger Ackroyd?" In *Classics and Commercials: A Literary Chronicle of the Forties*. New York: Farrar, Straus, Giroux, 1950, pp. 257–65.

Winnetka Graded Book List. Comp. Carleton Washburne and Mabel Vogel. Chicago: American Library Association, 1926.

Winks, Robin. *Modus Operandi: An Excursion into Detective Fiction.* Boston: Godine, 1982.

Yost, Edna. "The Fifty Cent Juveniles." *Publishers Weekly*, 18 June 1932, pp. 2405–08.

Zacharias, Lee. "Nancy Drew, Ballbuster." *Journal of Popular Culture*, 9 (1976), pp. 1027–38.

Zuckerman, Ed. "The Great Hardy Boys' Whodunit." *Rolling Stone*, 9 September 1976, pp. 36–40.

INDEX